Diving into Secure Access Service Edge

A technical leadership guide to achieving success with SASE at market speed

Jeremiah Ginn

BIRMINGHAM—MUMBAI

Diving into Secure Access Service Edge

Copyright © 2022 Packt Publishing

All rights reserved. No part of this book may be reproduced, stored in a retrieval system, or transmitted in any form or by any means, without the prior written permission of the publisher, except in the case of brief quotations embedded in critical articles or reviews.

Every effort has been made in the preparation of this book to ensure the accuracy of the information presented. However, the information contained in this book is sold without warranty, either express or implied. Neither the author, nor Packt Publishing or its dealers and distributors, will be held liable for any damages caused or alleged to have been caused directly or indirectly by this book.

Packt Publishing has endeavored to provide trademark information about all of the companies and products mentioned in this book by the appropriate use of capitals. However, Packt Publishing cannot guarantee the accuracy of this information.

Associate Group Product Manager: Mohd Riyan Khan

Publishing Product Manager: Shrilekha Malpani

Senior Editor: Shazeen Iqbal

Senior Content Development Editor: Adrija Mitra

Technical Editor: Nithik Cheruvakodan

Copy Editor: Safis Editing

Book Project Manager: Neil D'mello

Proofreader: Safis Editing

Indexer: Subalakshmi Govindhan

Production Designer: Alishon Mendonca

Marketing Coordinator: Ankita Bhonsle

First published: November 2022

Production reference: 1141022

Published by Packt Publishing Ltd.

Livery Place

35 Livery Street

Birmingham

B3 2PB, UK.

978-1-80324-217-0

www.packt.com

To my mother, Rachel Ginn, who taught me that every problem can be solved with hard work, kindness, and a genuine relationship with Jesus Christ.

– Jeremiah Ginn

Foreword

I had the privilege of meeting and working closely with *Jeremiah Ginn* in the successful deployment of a large SD-WAN solution for a top-tier AT&T customer. His forward-looking and thinking are unparalleled in this industry, and his leadership in the development process was exactly what we required to get this huge success. Jeremiah spends his time investing heavily in people both within the workplace and with his passions outside of the work environment.

Secure Access Service Edge (**SASE**) is one of the most widely used acronyms in the digital realm of all businesses and industries today. CEOs desire to understand it, CTOs desire to implement it, and security and network executives are working to deploy it. At the same time, engineering management and staff are actively creating lab scenarios and preparing for the upcoming shift they see coming at them. This book is directed at both those looking to be involved in SASE and those already heading down the path of SASE deployment.

Jeremiah is one of the leading and likely the most pervasive voices in the definition, design, and success of SASE. In this book, Jeremiah reveals the detailed success criteria necessary to meet the new level of challenges SASE creates, including the substantial executive support required and the paradigm shift in the training, implementation, maintenance, and support.

David H. Brown

Principal Architect at AT&T

Contributors

About the author

Jeremiah Ginn is a husband, father, teacher, engineer, architect, author, Cybersecurity Evangelist, children's advocate, advocate of Military Veterans and their families, and Service-Disabled Veteran who proudly served in the US Army. He currently has 11 children 3 biological, 6 adopted, and 2 in guardianship. Leading SDN evangelism efforts across many global organizations, his recent experience is in SD-WAN, SASE, NFV, multi-tenant cloud edge compute, and network infrastructure architecture, helping more than 3,000 organizations over the past 25 years. He contributes to the development of SDN, SD-WAN, and SASE solutions at AT&T. He is an IEEE member and contributes to The MEF Forum's W117 SASE Service Attributes and Service Framework.

Thank you to everyone that invested in me and my career. You know who you are! Thank you Meredith Ginn for the privilege of your hand in marriage for almost three decades. In five more decades, we should know enough about marriage to make an educated decision, but until then, I am happy to hold your hand. I love all of my children, regardless of how they came into my life, and regardless of what document signifies our relationship.

This is a technical book, a life book, an education book, a perspective book, and a lessons learned book. Thank you to David Brown, my technical reviewer and friend. Without David, this book could not have offered long-term value to those of us who learned engineering the old way.

Thank you to my team at Packt, who have worked incredibly hard to get this book to you. They probably all still have concerns about my approach to teaching as I am sure you will, but I hope this book helps you, your team, and your organization achieve the success that you truly deserve! Thank you for investing your personal time into reading this book as I wrote it to invest in you, the reader. May you be a perpetual learner and invest in other humans.

About the reviewer

David H. Brown is a Principal Architect at AT&T with decades of experience developing, managing, deploying, consulting and selling leading edge technologies to private and public companies. His professional experience as a trusted advisor has focused on enterprise solutions, deployment of information systems, and technology integration solutions for enterprise and government.

Previous to AT&T, David was a Principal Architect for VeriSign and has many years of experience working for small and large corporations and government organizations in full-time and consulting roles.

David holds multiple certifications, including CCIE #6231, CISSP #28504, GSEC #42081, and GCED #2487, and he also earned a master's degree (MBA) from McColl School at Queens University of Charlotte and a bachelor's degree in Computer Science from Le Moyne College.

David is a husband, father, and grandfather based in Charlotte, NC. Soli Deo Gloria.

I would like to heartily thank Jeremiah, the author of this book, for trusting me to review his work, and also my wife, Amy, for supporting me throughout my career to be in a position where my input matters.

Table of Contents

Preface	xiii

Part 1 – SASE Market Perspective

1

SASE Introduction — 3

Define SASE	3	Embrace SASE	7
Market SASE	4	Present SASE	8
Value SASE	6	Summary	10

2

SASE Human — 11

Human Issue	11	Human Solution	15
Human Problem	13	Human Patterns	16
Human Behavior	14	Summary	17

3

SASE Managed — 19

SASE Self	19	SASE Operational	23
SASE Co-managed	20	SASE Success	25
SASE Managed	21	Summary	26

4

SASE Orchestration — 27

SASE Manual	27	SASE Orchestrate	30
SASE Template	28	SASE Automate	32
SASE Integrate	30	Summary	33

5

SASE SD-WAN — 35

SD-What	35	SD-When	39
SD-Why	37	SD-SASE	39
SD-How	38	Summary	40

Part 2 – SASE Technical Perspective

6

SASE Detail — 43

Service Definition	44	Service Requirements	46
Service Components	45	Service Flight	47
Service Roles	46	Summary	49

7

SASE Session — 51

SASE Session	51	SASE Flow	54
SASE UNI	53	SASE Lifecycle	55
SASE Actors	53	Summary	56

8

SASE Policy — 57

SASE Policy	57	SASE Trust	61
SASE Quality	59	SASE Effective	61
SASE Dynamic	60	Summary	62

9

SASE Identity — 63

Access Identity	63	Situation Identity	66
Dimensional Identity	65	Integrate Identity	67
Context Identity	66	Summary	68

10

SASE Security — 71

Secure Overview	72	Secure Automation	75
Secure Details	73	Secure Summary	76
Secure Session	74	Summary	76

11

SASE Services — 77

Services Overview	78	Services Expanse	81
Services Core	79	Services Explain	82
Service Options	79	Summary	82

12

SASE Management — 85

Management Overview	86	Management Automation	90
Management Systems	88	Management Simplified	91
Management Templates	89	Summary	91

Part 3 – SASE Success Perspective

13

SASE Stakeholders — 95

Stakeholders Overview	96	Stakeholder Users	98
Stakeholders Business	96	Stakeholder Success	99
Stakeholders Technical	97	Summary	99

14

SASE Case — 101

Case Overview	101	Case Design	105
Case Insight	103	Case Value	107
Case Examples	103	Summary	108

15

SASE Design — 109

Design Overview	110	Design Support	113
Design Theory	112	Design Communication	114
Design Function	112	Summary	114

16

SASE Trust — 117

Zero Overview	118	Zero Trust	121
Zero Framework	118	Zero Explained	121
Zero Feed	120	Summary	122

Part 4 – SASE Bonus Perspective

17

SASE Learn — 125

Learn Overview	126	Learn Timing	131
Learn Model	127	Learn Explain	131
Learn Perpetual	130	Summary	132

18

SASE DevOps — 133

DevOps Overview	134	DevOps Act	138
DevOps Fervor	136	DevOps Impact	139
DevOps Continuous	137	Summary	139

19

SASE Forward — 141

Forward Overview	142	Forward Measured	145
Forward Present	143	Forward Concept	146
Forward Future	144	Summary	147

20

SASE Bonus — 149

SD-WAN Overview	150	SD-WAN Practice	155
SD-WAN Design	151	Summary	156
SD-WAN Failure	153	SASE Conclusion	156
SD-WAN Experience	154		

Appendix

SASE Terms — 157

Index — 163

Other Books You May Enjoy — 170

Preface

The SASE concept was coined by Gartner after seeing a pattern emerge in cloud and SD-WAN projects where full security integration was needed. The market behavior lately has sparked something like a "space race" for all technology manufacturers and cloud service providers to offer a "SASE" solution. The current training available in the market is minimal and manufacturer-oriented, with new services being released every few weeks. Professional architects and engineers trying to implement SASE need to take a manufacturer-neutral approach..

This guide provides a foundation for understanding SASE, but it also has a lasting impact because it not only addresses the problems that existed at the time of publication, but also provides a continual learning approach to successfully lead in a market that evolves every few weeks. Technology teams need a tool that provides a model to keep up with new information as it becomes available and stay ahead of market hype.

With this book, you'll learn about crucial models for SASE success in designing, building, deploying, and supporting operations to ensure the most positive **User Experience** (**UX**). In addition to SASE, you'll gain insight into SD-WAN design, DevOps, zero trust, and next-generation technical education methods.

Who this book is for

This book has been written for technology and security leaders, specifically CTOs, CSOs, CISOs, and CIOs who are looking for an executive approach to SASE for their organization. This book will help anyone implementing SD-WAN, SASE, and SASE services for cloud, network, and security infrastructure. It has been written with a market-central, vendor-agnostic approach beyond Gartner's ideas of SASE. SASE services are the path forward for secure communications for people, devices, applications, and systems to and from anywhere. This book is a challenge and call to action for anyone looking to improve their security, networking, and cloud success.

What this book covers

Chapter 1, *SASE Introduction*, introduces the term SASE, which was recently coined by Gartner and has been dominating IT projects to ensure cost savings and provide the needed security. The overall book provides a comprehensive foundational-level understanding of what SASE is, how to use SASE for success, how to learn through each evolution, where to find more information, and what the future of integrated secure access solutions looks like.

Chapter 2, SASE Human, discusses how understanding SASE requires a mix of skills not commonly found in one person. Due to the DevOps methodology's acceleration of software releases, a rapid approach to learning just-in-time prior implementation within two to six weeks is required for success. Miss the mark on this requirement and your employer ends up in the news for having the latest security failure in the market. Using a managed service provider that has multiple teams in lockstep with the developers allows an organization to pivot on demand, transfer liability, and meet the urgent needs of the organization on demand.

Chapter 3, SASE Managed, discusses how SASE is a different approach that requires the experience level of even the best engineers to be reset to zero. Once at zero, it can take 6 weeks or 6 months to achieve basic proficiency with design, implementation, and troubleshooting skills. This "retooling" of the engineering team within a non-technology-focused enterprise offers little value to shareholders or customers. Outsourcing to the right managed services partner allows the technology to provide business value much more quickly and change at the speed of the market.

Chapter 4, SASE Orchestration, looks at automated service management across potentially multiple operator networks, including fulfillment, control, performance, assurance, usage, security, analytics, and policy capabilities, which are achieved programmatically through APIs that provide abstraction from the network technology used to deliver the service.

Chapter 5, SASE SD-WAN, discusses SD-WAN, which provides a virtual overlay network that enables application-aware, policy-driven, and orchestrated connectivity between SD-WAN user network interfaces and provides the logical construct of an layer three, virtual private, routed network for the subscriber that conveys IP packets between subscriber sites.

Chapter 6, SASE Detail, deep dives into what makes a service SASE.

Chapter 7, SASE Session, looks at SASE sessions, which are the core component of a SASE solution. Connecting the target actor to the subject actor, regardless of connection type, in a secure session is the heart of SASE.

Chapter 8, SASE Policy, looks at SASE policies, which are sets of rules applied to the SASE session that can be integrated into SASE connectivity quality mechanisms as well as other SASE service inputs. In the past, policy-based firewall or routing solutions have been prescriptive, requiring a comprehensive understanding of the five Ws prior to implementation. The policy was written in stone to guarantee specific results. With SASE, a dynamic environment that allows machine interaction on demand is required for the service to offer a relevant value proposition. This environment is precursive to AI and has to be designed in a manner that allows for AIOps.

Chapter 9, SASE Identity, discusses how a multidimensional approach is required to integrate IAM, context, situational components, time of day, location, and many other factors to deliver sub-millisecond active security that is continuously relevant.

Chapter 10, SASE Security, discusses how each software product developer uses security vertically. In SASE sessions, these vertical solutions must integrate to form the pervasive security that is required for the solution.

Chapter 11, SASE Services, looks at how there are many services that can be included in a SASE service. Every service is not mandatory for a solution to be considered SASE, but every SASE service should have the ability to be integrated into an overall comprehensive solution for a secure connective solution. Potential example services for inclusion are listed in this chapter and are expected to evolve as this market matures.

Chapter 12, SASE Management, looks at establishing, monitoring, and enforcing the configuration, policy, and performance of any given component of or the overall SASE solution.

Chapter 13, SASE Stakeholders, discusses how the foundation for SASE solutions requires identifying all stakeholders in the end solution. Each stakeholder contributes to the cross-functional matrix approach in the project planning phase to qualifying security requirements.

Chapter 14, SASE Case, provides examples for educational purposes, but they are by no means "recipe cards" for implementation strategies or architectural blueprints. The Use Case in turn provides a model that allows for templated approaches that are necessary for scaling the ultimate solution.

Chapter 15, SASE Design, discusses how designing for SASE involves concepts relating to DevOps, security, SD-WAN, and the cloud, and displaces legacy LAN/WAN design principles primarily due to the disaggregation of data plane and control plane activity.

Chapter 16, SASE Trust, discusses the Zero Trust Framework, which is a cybersecurity architecture where all actors are authenticated, authorized, and continuously validated before subjects are granted access, maintain access to, or perform operations on targets.

Chapter 17, SASE Learn, discusses how SASE is a moving target that does not stop evolving. How do you learn something that is perpetually becoming more complex daily? How do you get ahead of the requirements? Where can you independently research this subject? We will provide answers to these questions in this chapter.

Chapter 18, SASE DevOps, discusses the DevOps mindset, which is a rigorous systematic, fervent approach to continual improvement through secure development iteration. Through iteration, the production release of code improves in security, reliability, and user experience.

Chapter 19, SASE Forward, discusses how the future of SASE will be completely different from today. But like the history of x86 computer hardware, it is somewhat predictable, and therefore, a pattern emerges that allows us to stay diligent and ahead of the next change.

Chapter 20, SASE Bonus, discusses how designing SD-WAN solutions is much more complex than a routed WAN with an identical scale. Multiple circuits across routers may be integrated by configuring a dynamic routing protocol that uses all available routes. In contrast, each SD-WAN path must be considered independently, and policies should be designed to give the orchestrator as much autonomy as possible in selecting the ideal path for each packet or flow.

To get the most out of this book

Software-defined technologies such as SD-WAN, SASE, and SDN are significantly different from the past four decades of network engineering. If you can accept this truth prior to reading this book, you may get more out of its content. This book is for those that want to deliver successful projects faster, further, and more cost-effectively than the market standard.

Conventions used

Bold: Indicates a new term, an important word, or words that you see onscreen. For instance, words in menus or dialog boxes appear in **bold**. Here is an example: "**SD-WAN** stands for **software-defined wide area network**."

> Tips or Important Notes
> Appear like this.

Get in touch

Feedback from our readers is always welcome.

General feedback: If you have questions about any aspect of this book, email us at customercare@packtpub.com and mention the book title in the subject of your message.

Errata: Although we have taken every care to ensure the accuracy of our content, mistakes do happen. If you have found a mistake in this book, we would be grateful if you would report this to us. Please visit www.packtpub.com/support/errata and fill in the form.

Piracy: If you come across any illegal copies of our works in any form on the internet, we would be grateful if you would provide us with the location address or website name. Please contact us at copyright@packt.com with a link to the material.

If you are interested in becoming an author: If there is a topic that you have expertise in and you are interested in either writing or contributing to a book, please visit authors.packtpub.com.

Share Your Thoughts

Once you've read *Diving into Secure Access Service Edge*, we'd love to hear your thoughts! Scan the QR code below to go straight to the Amazon review page for this book and share your feedback.

https://packt.link/r/1803242175

Your review is important to us and the tech community and will help us make sure we're delivering excellent quality content.

Download a free PDF copy of this book

Thanks for purchasing this book!

Do you like to read on the go but are unable to carry your print books everywhere?

Is your eBook purchase not compatible with the device of your choice?

Don't worry, now with every Packt book you get a DRM-free PDF version of that book at no cost.

Read anywhere, any place, on any device. Search, copy, and paste code from your favorite technical books directly into your application.

The perks don't stop there, you can get exclusive access to discounts, newsletters, and great free content in your inbox daily

Follow these simple steps to get the benefits:

1. Scan the QR code or visit the link below

https://packt.link/free-ebook/9781803242170

2. Submit your proof of purchase
3. That's it! We'll send your free PDF and other benefits to your email directly

Part 1 – SASE Market Perspective

Part 1 provides a basic understanding of SASE from the market perspective. This perspective is the required baseline prior to considering a SASE-related project. In this section, there are the following chapters:

- *Chapter 1, SASE Introduction*
- *Chapter 2, SASE Human*
- *Chapter 3, SASE Managed*
- *Chapter 4, SASE Orchestration*
- *Chapter 5, SASE SD-WAN*

1
SASE Introduction

Recently coined by *Gartner*, **Secure Access Service Edge** (**SASE**) has been dominating **Information Technology** projects for both cost savings and needed pervasive security. This book provides a comprehensive foundational level understanding of what SASE is, how to leverage SASE for success, how to learn through each evolution, where to find more information, and what the future of integrated secure access solutions looks like.

We will begin this by introducing the concept of SASE for those who are still trying to clarify what SASE is or *what it is not*. In this chapter, we will cover how the market is defining SASE, what the actual market is for SASE, why we need to embrace SASE, and how to present SASE to your organization in a comprehensive manner.

In this chapter, we're going to cover the following main topics:

- Define SASE—what SASE is and what SASE is not
- Market SASE—a market evaluation of SASE
- Value SASE—value proposition, SASE services
- Embrace SASE—embracing the idea of a SASE framework
- Present SASE—presenting the idea of SASE and clearing the hype cycle

Define SASE

SASE is pronounced *sassy*. Andrew Lerner at *Gartner* coined the phrase in a blog post on December 23, 2019. That post can be found at `https://blogs.gartner.com/andrew-lerner/2019/12/23/say-hello-sase-secure-access-service-edge/`. He explains that **Software-Defined Wide Area Network** (**SD-WAN**) needed a security package. SD-WAN effectively replaces router-based WAN solutions in a next-generation software based package.

The SD-WAN solution varies from vendor to vendor but incorporates secure data forwarding with policies that leverage application specifications to guarantee the best handling of traffic for each application. This improves the **User Experience** (**UX**) as well as the network's resilience.

We now refer to SASE as a *framework*. SASE leverages multiple security services into a framework approach. Not all services offered as SASE solutions are required to be compliant, but adherence to a comprehensive security framework approach is expected. Currently, there is no SASE certification; instead, most of the SASE hype comes from intense competition through effective marketing.

The idea of SASE was not far from what security consultants were already doing by integrating multiple security solutions into a stack that ensured a comprehensive, layered, secure access solution. This approach is something I was already doing for my customers in ensuring **Next-Generation Firewall (NGFW)**, **Intrusion Detection System (IDS)**, **Intrusion Prevention System (IPS)**, and other necessary security solutions were a part of every SD-WAN installation. By calling it a SASE framework, the approach to a comprehensive solution somehow felt more focused than what the industry recognized as just a best security practice.

Commonly, SASE services include **SD-WAN**, **Zero-Trust Network Access (ZTNA)**, **Cloud Access Security Broker (CASB)**, **NGFW**, **Secure Web Gateway (SWG)**, unified management, and orchestration. Just what constitutes a *real SASE solution* varies greatly by source. Several organizations, such as the **Metro Ethernet Forum (MEF)**, are trying to establish neutral industry standards for SASE. These standards will pave the way for a universal understanding, the ability to integrate multiple manufacturers into a solution, and a method for teaching SASE.

Most network communications and security vendors have been working to create a full SASE framework under their brand. Their marketing presents the idea that a full SASE solution from a single vendor is the way to ensure security. Current customer feedback from the *Fortune 500* class of NCE link" businesses is that two to three **Original Equipment Manufacturer (OEM)** vendors will need to be integrated to allow for *best-of-breed* solutions. This provides an opportunity for a **Managed Service Provider (MSP)** to give orchestration across multiple platforms to achieve optimal security.

To summarize, SASE is a new, next-generation secure communications services framework that combines many different services to close previous gaps in security. In the next section, we will define the market as it pertains to SASE services and solutions.

Market SASE

In the market today, a few different manufacturers offer self-proclaimed SASE products. The potential list of services across their portfolios that may be a part of a complete SASE service could be in the dozens, depending on their market approach. Calling a service SASE does not make it so, and as there is no SASE certification for solutions at the time of writing this book, no vendor or MSP is exclusively accurate in their marketing of what is or is not SASE. The standards for SASE have not been published at this time.

Gartner started a fire with that simple blog post in 2019. Overnight, every SD-WAN solution in the market offered a path to SASE. The SASE idea itself multiplied the SD-WAN market's potential revenue of over $11 billion **United States Dollars (USD)** by 2028. The global secure access service edge (SASE) market size is expected to reach $11.29 billion USD by 2028, registering a CAGR of 36.4%, a ResearchAndMarkets report reveals. The source of this quotation can be found at the following link: `https://www.helpnetsecurity.com/2021/08/17/sase-market-2028/`.

The reality is that an $11 billion-dollar market is only the core SASE product offering for the market. **Hardware**, **software licensing**, **hosting**, **maintenance**, and **support** make up the core products, whereas managed services and professional services can multiply the market impact by up to 25 times the core product revenue.

Market Challenge

The market challenge for realizing revenue potential will be primarily impacted negatively by a lack of skilled labor for design, build, and deploy services. This skills gap and the operational expenses preference of most **Chief Information Officer/Chief Financial Officer** (**CIO/CFO**) strategies will drive more than 70% of the market to contract SASE as a managed services offering. In the market, there is a trend of up to 78% of SD-WAN contracts leveraging managed services as opposed to utilizing in-house engineering teams. The primary reason for this change is not tied to SASE as CIO and CFO focus has been to rely on technical services as **Operating Expense** (**OPEX**) as opposed to **Capital Expense** (**CAPEX**). OPEX has been the goal for what is considered by an organization as non-business value cost. Generally, the CIO direction of the largest organizations is to convert operational support staff costs in order to leverage the cost savings on **Software Development combined with IT Operations** (**DevOps**) staff costs, which can offer a business **Return On Investment** (**ROI**). Support teams are a cost center, whereas the DevOps team can provide the potential to be a profit center to the company.

The complexity of SASE services is driving the need for technology engineering careers to move to a continual learning path. The time has passed where an engineer could rest on traditional education or certification paths. Traditional academic education can provide perspective, historical knowledge, foundational knowledge, and soft skills required for functioning in an organizational environment, whereas industry and manufacturing certifications provide core technical knowledge for functional understanding in a vertical role within an organization. Both educational methods are beneficial for building a foundational understanding of a skill set and both are effective filters when recruiting for a specific role. Unfortunately, neither can move at a market pace, which is today at an average of three DevOps or **Software Development combined with Security and IT Operations** (**DevSecOps**) sprint cycles from being out of date and ineffective.

Software development follows a continual improvement path, and so must its practitioners. The goal of the DevOps mentality is to leverage iterative development in a modular fashion as opposed to legacy, ground-up development and **Go-To-Market** (**GTM**) practices. DevOps practitioners continually develop, improve, and release. **Scrum sprint cycles** vary by organization, but an average of 2 weeks can be used as a model to understand the phases of development. New network and security software releases are no longer tied to hardware releases as they can function as a **Virtual Machine** (**VM**), **Virtual Network** (**VNet**) function, cloud-native function, application, or service independent of a platform. The entire GTM process could be as little as one Scrum sprint cycle or 2 weeks. Network and security practitioners operate on a **New -1** (**N-1**) basis, N-1+validated, or wait for a triggering event to validate a new software release. The market average for consumption of new software releases is moving to an average of three sub-versions of code, which could average 6 weeks between the last production upgrade of software and the next production upgrade.

The market has been slow to admit that network or security engineering is no longer a discrete skill set from software development. In fact, SASE services will receive major software updates every 2 to 6 weeks, depending on the development cycle or security issues with each independent SASE service within the overall solution. Minor updates may occur in real time. Education for engineering teams must align with software release cycles.

In summary, the market's perception of SASE varies according to the beholder's skill set. As a result of rapid product development, the market for SASE is likely to grow exponentially, creating the issue of rapid evolution that needs to be managed. The next section clarifies the value proposition of a SASE framework for secure communication solutions.

Value SASE

Effective security is inherently valuable, but how do we accurately estimate that value? How do we quantify the value of a solution for an unknown risk impact? Former President of the US, Ronald Reagan, was quoted as saying: "*Information is the oxygen of the modern time. It seeps through the walls topped by barbed wire; it wafts across the electrified borders.*" If information is oxygen, what is the accurate value of oxygen to human life? Effective security pays for itself in reducing risk, liability, and loss of unknown quantities by protecting that oxygen or—in this case—non-public information.

To evaluate SASE in a value proposition or ROI, the investment should be first quantified. Steven Ross, Executive Principal of *Risk Masters Inc.*, points to the **Return on Security Investment** (**ROSI**), which is a calculable assessment as a way of identifying the monetary value of the security investment. This may be important to the CFO or investors as a model for understanding financially the inherent value of secure IT investments. More information can be found at the following link: `https://www.isaca.org/resources/isaca-journal/past-issues/2011/what-is-the-value-of-security#1`.

Without effective security solutions, an organization will cease to achieve a primary ROI for time and capital invested. A recommended value proposition for security is the ability to conduct, without obstruction, the primary business of the organization on whose behalf the secure solution is employed. SASE provides cost-effective security and builds value by reducing inefficiencies in previously developed generations of secure communications. Cost reductions can be achieved by reducing labor, time, capital, focus, outages, performance issues, and educational requirements for staff members trying to build their own perfect technology. Simply speaking, the investment required to develop secure technology solutions in-house with homegrown or *best-of-breed* market solutions has been providing a negative ROI, which has driven the market to leverage an MSP that specializes in a specific technology. This method also allows for the transfer of liability to the MSP, which provides some relief for executives not choosing to develop their own secure communications solution in-house.

Leveraging SASE with SD-WAN prepares networking and security solutions for a future of automated and secure IT provisioning with real-time operations remediation. To eliminate the inefficiencies that every network has experienced, the solution starts with abstracted components and the disaggregation of data and control-plane activity (separating components). By leveraging a deconstructive process, smaller changes may be made, reducing the risk of any one change causing a major impact to secure network communications. The smaller the change, the quicker the change can provide business value. The target process is analogous to a garden-pruning process that makes small changes until the overall desired effect is achieved. Unlike physical garden pruning, small changes in SASE can be reversed quickly if a negative outcome is realized. Overall, this methodology allows IT organizations to move much quickly than we could even 5 years ago, which allows us to do more with less at the pace of the market.

Orchestration allows for solutions to be templated. The orchestrator allows templates to be overlain upon any of the logical components in the overall solution or service. The creation of a template-based design offers rapid deployment across the abstracted solution. An additional benefit of orchestration is that template continuity may be enforced by the orchestrator and any variance in behavior be reported to security operations systems for tracking and mitigation. This process allows the achievement of compliance with approved network or security designs and immediately identifies violations for action.

SASE provides value in efficiencies, scale, automation, enforcement, and orchestration over similar secure communications technologies in production today. The overall value reduces the design, build, deploy, and operate labor required to keep an organization communicating securely.

Overall, the value of a SASE solution lies in its ability to reduce productivity losses caused by security risks or threats. SASE integrates independent security solutions for a holistic approach that can be automated, reducing the amount of human labor required while taming a mission that was once near impossible.

In the following section, I hope that you will learn to embrace SASE for the inherent benefits it provides to your organization.

Embrace SASE

SD-WAN adoption was extremely slow from inception and into 2021. The main reason for the slow adoption was due to a lack of education prior to intense market demand, based on inflated cost-savings estimates over **Multiprotocol Label Switching** (**MPLS**) and other legacy network types. *Gartner* defined the **Gartner Hype Cycle** as a method for evaluating when to leverage a **New-to-Market** (**NTM**) technology. In their five phases, they identify levels of understanding a shiny new market idea prior to consumption. The benefit of this approach is that it gives the perspective necessary to make an educated decision. More information is available at the following link: `https://www.gartner.com/en/research/methodologies/gartner-hype-cycle`.

Educated decisions require available educational material, which doesn't materialize in the market until the *Trough of Disillusionment*. Phase three is roughly where the lessons learned are documented and an effective curriculum is developed, allowing training to start. At the time of writing this book, the *Hype Cycle* for SASE is still effectively in phase one, where there is much more excitement than factual data.

The promise of SASE is tied to the value; faster, easier, more secure, more automation, and rapid deployment. *Better, faster, and cheaper* is the market's battle cry. A well-designed SASE can deliver on all these when paired with the right resources. The correct mindset is that security is done in layers, and the best security leverages as many layers as is productionally sound. The best security does not come from a product but through best-practice frameworks implemented correctly. The qualified resource can come from networking, security, or software backgrounds, but is the continually self-educating resource that is concerned about being right for the sake of those served, as opposed to being right for the sake of righteousness. There is no *silver bullet* for solving the resource/ market/skills gap; however, the right resources will self-educate perpetually, allowing themselves to be wrong in knowledge so that they can remediate their gap and their solution will be right in production.

In conclusion, SASE helps organizations reduce their ongoing labor investments in security operations after initial design and implementation. While embracing SASE will take a significant investment of time, it will provide significant returns.

The next section will provide you with an outline for a comprehensive presentation on SASE that can be tailored to your target audience.

Present SASE

Presenting SASE to executive, administrative, or technical audiences requires a framework for discussion, of which a sample is provided in the following list of items, with a key understanding of each topic that may be further detailed or placed into a slide format with speaker notes:

1. **Introduction:**

    - SASE is pronounced *sassy*.
    - *Gartner* defined the term to describe what was happening in the market.
    - SASE services may include SD-WAN, ZTNA, CASB, NGFW, SWG, as well as other services.

2. **From Framework to Managed Service:**

    - The SASE framework provides for the integration of solutions from multiple vendors.
    - The market is buying SASE services on a consumption basis.
    - Most organizations will leverage two to three SASE vendors and one MSP.

3. **SASE Managed Service:**

    - This effective managed service offering allows for OPEX instead of CAPEX.
    - Managed services are being consumed for SASE due to rapid software development ahead of effective education for engineering or operations staff.

- The right managed service offering provides orchestration, open **Application Programming Interface (API)** integration, **Artificial Intelligence for IT Operations (AIOps)**, and multivendor seamless integration.

4. **SASE Service Stakeholders:**

    - For secure, compliant, resilient, and high-performing solutions, a framework for feedback and participation in business-impacting decisions is required.
    - Stakeholders may be defined leveraging **Project Management Institute-Project Management Professional (PMI-PMP)** best practice.
    - Governance is required.

5. **Actors and the Managed Service:**

    - SASE defines subject actors, target actors, and the role MSPs play.
    - A *subscriber* contracts a service for the actor's benefit.
    - The managed service must provide layers of security that account for real-time access to zero trust.

6. **Identity, Context, Situation:**

    - *Identity*, as in who or what is authorized by the service.
    - *Situation* builds upon the context for the access role and further defines access.

7. **SASE Sessions:**

    - Sessions are the heart of SASE and may be considered as a wrapper for network sessions.
    - Sessions incorporate application-specific policies.
    - Sessions leverage the zero-trust framework as well as SD-WAN.

8. **SASE Security:**

    - Security is not a product but builds effective layers upon a secure foundation.
    - DevSecOps and DevOps necessitate production software code updates as often as every 2 weeks.
    - SASE will require integration across vendors for *best-of-breed* capabilities.

9. **SASE Policies:**

    - Legacy firewall or router policies force specific behaviors that are not sensitive to external changes in the factors by which that policy was written.

    - Automation and orchestration allow policies to be changed based on real-time conditions.

    - Effective SASE policy considers all available data in the decision process.

10. **SASE Connectivity:**

    - Most commonly, SASE connectivity will come from SD-WAN.

    - SD-WAN allows SASE to leverage quality, performance, and application-awareness tools.

    - Remote access solutions, **Fifth-Generation Cellular** (5G) services, satellite services, Ethernet circuits, and legacy WANs may be incorporated into SASE.

11. **SASE Services Use Csases:**

    - The primary SASE use case is SD-WAN plus security.

    - SASE may be leveraged for both cloud infrastructure and applications.

    - SASE can be used to create on-demand, secure communications across any network type.

12. **Looking Forward:**

    - The future is SASE, as it is possibly the last step in the *pure cloud* transformation journey that all organizations must take.

    - AIOps with SASE allows for consistent, reliable, secure, and on-demand application access.

    - SASE education must follow the continual learning, continual improvement path for staff.

Presenting SASE requires a balance between the past, present, and future, as well as between many independent technology focus areas. This outline provided a framework for bringing the entire audience into a SASE mindset, regardless of skill set.

Summary

In this chapter, we've provided an overview of SASE with a definition of it, as well as the original concept that was coined by *Gartner*. We evaluated the market for SASE services. SASE's value was discussed, as well as the importance of embracing SASE to obtain returns on security investments. Toward the end of the chapter, we offered an outline by which SASE can be presented as a whole concept to an audience.

In the next chapter, we will be covering SASE as it relates to the *Human* element. We will cover the Issue, Problem, Behaviors, Solution, and Pattern of Humans in the SASE world. The *SASE Human* chapter will help leaders form thought leadership as it relates to their staff and SASE programs for their organization.

2
SASE Human

Understanding **Secure Access Service Edge** (**SASE**) requires a mix of skills not commonly found in one person. Due to **Software Development combined with IT Operations** (**DevOps**) methodology, a rapid approach to learning is required. Effective training must be delivered **Just-in-Time** (**JIT**), prior to implementation. The training cannot follow the formal model but instead must be developed and delivered within two to six week increments parallel to, and in conjunction with, the software release. Miss the mark on this requirement and your employer ends up in the news as the latest security failure on the market.

Leveraging a **Managed Service Provider** (**MSP**) that has multiple DevOps teams in lockstep with the primary software developers allows an organization to pivot on-demand, transfer liability, and meet the urgent needs of the organization on-demand.

In this chapter, we will discuss the isue, problem, behavior, and solution that is *human*, and we will dig into the pattern that must evolve with the market; otherwise, success may never be possible.

We are going to cover the following main topics in this chapter:

- Human Issue – understand the issue
- Human Problem – state the problem
- Human behavior – identify the behavior
- Human Solution – develop the solution
- Human Patterns – change the patterns

Human Issue

The human issue with SASE is that human learning has a framework incompatible with the pace of the market. The previous model for software development was the *waterfall* or *linear* project plan that allowed for the distribution of work between teams of various skills. Inevitably, each team worked at different paces, with different approaches to solving challenges in their portion of the project. As the project timeline passed through each phase of development, the would-be product became more incompatible, which required significant labor, time, cost, and testing to resolve the issues.

The standard approach, while comfortable to skilled humans, consistently fails to meet the intersections of cost and market timing to be an effective *killer app*, while lighter and less feature-rich, inferior products hit the market in a massively profitable manner. These lesser products run proverbial circles around the more robust, correctly designed, appropriately staffed, and well-funded product. The better product, which is close to perfection, fails to break even financially, and it missed the sweet spot in the market demand curve. It missed the market timing due to the rigid pursuit of unattainable product perfection and therefore cost the developer's company their quarter, their year, or their entire business. Technology and business professionals have loved many of these companies because of their pursuit of perfection and their great products, but the love did not save the company from financial insolvency.

More than 20 years ago, Bill Gates taught us a valuable lesson through Microsoft. The market generally buys at approximately 85% of perfection, and if the product is good enough, customers are happy to take an initial working release and accept updates to solve any issues. Many of the great software companies that customers have loved over the years have disappeared through bankruptcy or undervalued acquisitions. This was due to the pursuit of 100%-perfect software-based products. Product perfection, especially software development, is not an achievable goal. If we can admit that perfection is unattainable at any price and that the market buys at 85% of perfection, then we can start to achieve profitability through effective product development by striving for market release in the 85-95%-perfection range.

The good news is that we find a premium can be added for every additional 1% of perfection, added to the market target of 85%. For instance, a product at 87% sells well, and the same product at 92% can achieve a 20% premium over the junior offering. Often, the most expensive software packages boast of a 99.99% service level but are often in the 95-97% range, and essentially provide liability management through a premium warranty. Many of these products rapidly resolve software issues within a few days of identification, either by the customer or the developer community.

Regardless of the actual methodology or philosophy leveraged for software development practices, most software development teams refer to their process as **Agile** because they work in short bursts of time – commonly known as **Sprint Cycles**. Each sprint cycle can last 2 to 6 weeks on average and produces one iteration of software code. Depending on the organization, that could be a fully functional product or a sub-component of a product. The general goal is one of **Continuous Integration and Continuous Delivery**, which is referred to as **CI/CD**. The **D** in *CD*, however, could be *development*, *deployment*, *delivery*, or another organizational-specific designation. The **I** is mostly referred to as *integration*, but should also be considered as *iteration*.

The process of iteration is one by which the market learned to create something useful that works today and can be used today. After feedback on the working product, that feedback is put into the next sprint cycle for a much-improved product to be released at the end of the cycle. Ideally, this process of iteration produces an initial working product within six weeks of inception and delivers an improved version of that product every two to six weeks. `Scrum.org` teaches the ideas behind this methodology, which, for many, has become a core philosophy in the way they approach any issue in life: *Do something, get feedback, do something better, repeat!* For additional information, review the Agile Manifesto at `https://resources.scrumalliance.org/Article/key-values-principles-agile-manifesto`.

In summary, the human issue with SASE is that meaningful changes in software, hardware, services, and communications are being brought to market in an *as-available* method that must be securely integrated into the production **SASE Service on-Demand**. A basic SASE solution will incorporate at least five different services and may include more than 100 different services. Each of the services in the overall solution will have different sprint cycles, which means that every two to six weeks, new software code is being delivered that must work with the overall SASE service.

In the next section, we will explore the problem with any human regarding education.

Human Problem

The human problem is that we cannot learn enough about dozens, or potentially hundreds, of secure communications products every two to six weeks to make effective decisions about what to upgrade, when to upgrade, the risk of upgrading, or the risk of not upgrading a particular product. Orchestration, automation, templating, and **Artificial Intelligence** (**AI**) built into operational support models can reduce the amount of human labor required to scale SASE. The progress that the technology market has made in reducing the labor required to deliver a secure communications solution at scale is extremely beneficial, and it is tangible. Unfortunately, it requires skills not effectively taught at this time to design, build, deploy, and operate. These skills must be *human*, and the first step taken must be *human*. The iteration of the solution must be *human* too. Technology can reduce the human requirement, but cannot eliminate all labor requirements, ethically or soon.

The primary problem is education. This problem ties back to the traditional academic model of education. At some point, every society needed formal education to allow for common communication within society. The next educational layer was the idea of *the Renaissance*, where diversity of educational topics developed a well-rounded individual, increased peaceful communication, reduced war in general, and prepared the world for collaboration. In addition to a well-rounded education, broad education combined with some specialization allowed masters of their skills to both develop and communicate their achievements. A master skilled individual's early marketing achievements inspired further achievements, increasing both global and common knowledge at the same time. The idea of a free and common education allowed the *Industrial Revolution* and its achievements to bring us into a modern era of cost-effective, commonly available resources for all of society.

In the current era, there is a major gap between the availability of resources with an effective education in the requisite skill set to align market needs with humans to perform needed functions. The educated human workforce is skilled for jobs that have been disappearing due to changing markets, and jobs that are in demand have no *effective* education to prepare humans to provide consistent value. The global job market continues to maintain openings for jobs that educational systems and human preferences provide inadequate quantities of workers for. This gap in supply and demand of employees creates an escalation of labor costs, as well as rapid movement between employers, known as *job-hopping*, for effectively-skilled workers.

Perhaps the past 30 years of *digital revolution* have exacerbated the issue of educational reform as the gap between market and education continues to grow. Humans that possess the necessary market skills are extensively self-educated. Often, those skilled developers that are developing the necessary software code for key contributions are not even primary-school graduates but instead began coding at an early age and launched multiple products prior to adulthood. Most software developers have college degrees, but the next generation of software start-up founders or security geniuses may be as young as 10 years old in an ever-evolving landscape. Achievement is not bound by age or status; instead, it is inherently meritorious.

What is the difference in approach between that of a child and that of a mature adult that causes the child to learn through curiosity and the adult to require rigor? The difference could be a lack of an established framework in the child's mind. The child learns naturally from birth, whereas the adult follows a socially acceptable process that is indoctrinated through formal education. However, without possessing an educational framework from traditional educational models to govern the educational approach, the child develops an improvised, self-developed method for learning. The child is accepting of knowledge from all available sources and tests that education through trial and error, with little fear of failure. This is a naturally occurring process that is slowly removed by formal training.

It could be that formal frameworks established in formal educational institutions look at the problem in a global, societal, solution framework. This global approach must account for all humans and must encourage non-conforming components of the system into compliance to measure effectiveness. Science teaches us that we must be able to measure progress to validate that progress has been achieved.

The market teaches evolutional behavior in value. If value becomes a moving target, then scientific measurement must follow the pace of evolutionary change. Multi-year statistical models become ineffective in a market evolving in a millisecond-based time sequence. The **User Experience (UX)** with any software-based cloud service is measured in milliseconds. The financial benefits of any software-based cloud service are paid in line with the UX.

In summary, the problem is *the human*. Humans follow conditioning that is developed over a significant passage of time. As with the evolution of that conditioning, reconditioning requires a similar timetable to that of the present level of conditioning. Currently, humans are not capable of keeping up with the current pace of secure communications technology on an individual basis.

In the next section, we will review how human behavior that is applied through effective reward systems achieves its desired goals.

Human Behavior

Generally, human behavior follows an informal cost/benefit analysis that can be compared to formal corporate analysis prior to planning meetings for the following year's budget. Despite common knowledge that humans work for reasons beyond financial benefits, consistent corporate behavior ignores the correlation. Organizations continue to hire at market rates, overtask their workers, underdevelop them, and expect great things from humans while effectively mistreating the *most valuable assets* of their organization. This corporate behavior is largely human in nature and is consistently disappointed that the conditioned behavior nets similar results to previously attempted versions of the same plan.

The brain performance of the average human is amazing and is virtually consumed by non-essential tasking. The ability to leverage the performance capacity available exists and is available on-demand. The human allocates this capacity for those tasks that have the highest immediate reward. When discipline is used, allocation to a combination of tasks that offer rewards for short, intermediate, and long-term benefits is possible. A common understanding of human behavior in this matter can make repetitive demands from a human offensive without compensating them appropriately for corporate outcomes through effective reward systems. A model for corrective reward systems tied to achieving specific target outcomes could leverage **Scrum**. Scrum's approach to product development could be leveraged and refined as a process directing human performance. Instead of a software product, the target goal would be human achievement as the product.

By leveraging rewards systems and clear measurable goals, behavior can be measured and, consequently, improved. Unacceptable behavior is a result of conditioning through causation and decisions made regarding risk/reward, cost/benefit, or other potential factors. Exceptionally positive behavior is similar in so much that each decision slightly tunes the behavior into an outcome above the desired goal. Effective reward systems account for human behavior and match the reward with the stated or desired outcome. The effect is similar to a video game that rewards a player for a specific achievement and then graduates that player to the next level after a pattern of success. The video game provides instant feedback on behavior, and the player adjusts their behavior to achieve rewards.

In summary, if change is required, the natural process cannot be ignored. The timeline to effect change in behavior is much like the timeline that created the current behavior. A chart documenting complete change in behavior typically shows the fast method and the slow method of change arriving at a complete change in behavior at approximately the same time. In other words, there are no shortcuts for effective changes in human behavior. Trying to accelerate human behavior is the subject of many horror movies.

In the next section, we find that not only is the human element the issue or problem, but it is also the solution.

Human Solution

The solution is the **Human**, but the human solution will not be easily developed or implemented. Identifying, acknowledging, and admitting the fact of the issue or problem is the first step in the process. To reach a resolution, actualization must occur to determine that a solution is needed. Humans are capable of positive change. In the world of ever-evolving technology, a major change must take place to achieve a level of understanding that allows for secure communications systems. We simply are not creating skilled humans who can meet the needs of emerging technologies such as SASE and those that follow.

The solution is to approach education in the same way that DevOps practices CI/CD on a per-sprint-cycle basis. This model could be described as *JIT* education. Essentially, the education could be an embedded object in a newly released software that, when activated by the human in question, could walk through a primer on the release notes and how that would impact the decisions necessary to integrate with other solutions. Often, a short *how-to video* with short textual references solves minor gaps in understanding. Solving this problem may just require an additional sense of purpose development in those types of activities. A fancy, future version of this idea may be an **Augmented Reality (AR)** solution with task overlay content showing risk/reward patterns on each decision made by the technology practitioner. This method may be further accelerated through conversational AI systems.

The solution is iterative education delivered as near to the need as possible. The framework could be taught in formal settings in conjunction with DevOps or DevSecOps processes. Once the foundation is set, then short incremental education can build on it, not just layer by layer as it has in the past. The educational build process must not pay homage to the foundation but correct mistakes that were made as new knowledge becomes available. Identifying and correcting mistakes with each iteration is the core of CI.

Often, identifying a mistake in a professor's foundational principles can feel irreverent, as that person may have contributed significantly to who you have become. It should feel the opposite, as professors take pride in providing their students with a framework for life and a pursuit of the best version of it. The altruist goal of the educator expects the student to build upon the foundation not from blind loyalty, but for the benefit and betterment of others. This investment into those educated by the educator should blossom and grow by way of innovation. That innovation includes improving the educator's foundation, built in the student's mind for all humans to benefit from.

Effective education for emerging technology should be a demand of the consumer or practitioner. All educational components must be modular and focus on the practical application of the topic. Formal education provides theory and methodology, and this model must not abstract from vocational aspects that lead to secure consumption of the software.

The solution is the improvement of practical education with every iteration of product development. Just as the software-based product must improve per iteration, so must the education that has been incorporated with the product. Human life is improved through iteration, trial, error, practical application of attained knowledge, and above all, mistakes. Making mistakes is not a comfortable experience but may be one of the most valuable learning tools. A mistake in a previous iteration must be corrected, and the mistake itself must be shared in the next iteration of the educational module.

In summary, the solution is the **Human**! In the next section, we will explore patterns in human behavior.

Human Patterns

Patterns may be easily observed in nature. Patterns may bring comfort to both the human observing and the human participating in these patterns. Patterns may be both positive and negative, good, bad, creative, destructive, relaxing, and terrifying. Ultimately, a pattern can be described as two opposite states at the same time. Once understood, patterns may be leveraged for either general or specific outcomes. In the human world, a pattern can often be referred to as a *habit*. In the context of discussion for SASE, a pattern may be thought of as a series of habits that can be collectively described as human behavior.

A pattern can be made, changed, broken, employed, copied, seen, heard, and felt. Each human has an aggregate pattern, and that pattern has an infinite number of customizations available. If that pattern becomes one of continual improvement through education, trial, and error, then there are potentially no limits to that human's achievement. Together, there are no limits to what a collection of human achievers may accomplish.

SASE specifically will continue to evolve every 2 to 6 weeks, requiring the human team designing, building, implementing, and supporting it to evolve their knowledge at the same pace. The services included in a SASE solution will multiply. Today, the market will identify 5-17 services as SASE *core services*, and individual SASE service vendors may claim over 100 different services in their *full SASE* product set. SASE is not a product but a framework for achieving secure communications. What is being communicated with will continue to evolve. It is easy to say **Software-Defined Wide Area Network (SD-WAN)**, remote access for computer users, cloud-based applications, and standard uses of network or security solutions are SASE. In actuality, SASE is the approach to ensuring all applications, regardless of the communications mechanism, are securely communicated with. This approach elevates SASE to a living status where it will grow and evolve as it matures.

SASE education *must* parallel and support the software release cycles in real time. New SASE practitioners or operators must change their approach to education and become childlike in their curiosity to explore each adjacent topic, developing their own individual CI/CD education. When we reinvent our learning approach to mirror that of our early childhood self, we see what we could not have seen before. We become able to identify what we did not know at this point. In doing so, we now understand our gap in understanding, and we become able to start resolving that gap. We can develop a plan and act on it with *the fact of the matter*. We can give ourselves permission to start from the beginning once we know where the beginning is. An established beginning allows for measured progress.

Human patterns must evolve at market pace to be effective. The pattern can be improved and targeted to meet the need, and the reward system must align with the need and must not diminish the value. As goals target the needs and corrected reward systems align with those goals, the human becomes the solution!

Summary

In this chapter, we covered the issue, problem, behavior, and solution that is uniquely human. By understanding the human pattern, it may be evaluated and tailored for desired outcomes. The aim is to correct the pattern and achieve the value of the corrected outcome. If you ignore the pattern, the consequence will be a failure to achieve the desired outcomes and may include further catastrophic results.

We must change our approach to education to match the world's needs or become extinct. Our existing systems of learning, while effective at creating an interoperating society, are ineffective at solving evolution needs. By adjusting education to become light, iterative, JIT, on-demand, and targeted, we increase human evolutionary effectiveness. This approach can eliminate market surplus in workers with misaligned skill sets and repurpose those workers for market demand-based roles. This educational solution works both for strategic and tactical roles.

In the next chapter, *SASE Managed*, we will be explaining what a SASE management model looks like, with sections on *Self, CO-Managed, and Managed models*. We will also identify effective operational and overall SASE Success models.

3
SASE Managed

SASE is a different approach that requires the experience level of the best engineers to be reset to zero. It is time to start the educational process over and set aside pride to humbly achieve SASE success. Once at zero, the process can take six weeks to six months to achieve basic proficiency with design, implementation, and troubleshooting skills. Unless your organization is an infrastructure or network security software developer as your primary revenue source, an ROI will not be forthcoming, and re-tooling the network and security engineering team offers little value to shareholders or customers. Outsourcing to the correct **Managed Services Partner** (**MSP**) allows the technology to provide business value much more quickly and allows the technology to change at the speed of the market.

In this chapter, we will discuss management topics, basic management models, the value of each management model, how to make SASE effective to scale, and the sub-components needed to scale.

We are going to cover the following main topics in this chapter:

- SASE Self – what does it mean to self-manage SASE
- SASE Co-managed – what does it mean to co-manage SASE
- SASE Managed – what does it mean to consume managed SASE
- SASE Operational – what does it mean to operate SASE
- SASE Success – what does it mean to achieve SASE success

SASE Self

Self-managed, meaning management by the end user organization of a SASE framework-based solution is a *fool's errand*. Put simply, SASE is one of the few skills within IT work where the *do it yourself* approach can cost exponentially more than the outsourced model. SASE services may include between 1 and 100 different services that require perpetual education with experience at scale. This may be the first technology in 60 years that 90% of all organizations will need to outsource to a managed services provider.

Consuming a single SASE service starts in the same way as acquiring a new firewall vendor. If an organization pivots from one brand firewall to another, the education process is simple. The idea would be to send security engineering and support staff members for formal training and require certification of their skills. The SASE version of that solution will require education milestones on top of the base certification at least every six weeks while the product is in service.

Compounding the educational requirements for *self-managed* service models, the average SASE service will include five core services and may consume more than 15 separate services. To be effective, the staff supporting SASE must specialize in three to five services to keep up with the pace of software releases from each service. A dedicated testing team will be necessary for cross-service testing prior to production for each release. A cloud sandbox for service testing must be established with strict control protocols for testing the interoperation between each service in production. Workshops prior to upgrades every few weeks will require cross-specialization mapping of integrated services to ensure that no new change impacts either the performance or security of the overall SASE service.

In summary, the self-managed model for SASE is only an option for companies willing to invest in DevSecOps teams, tools, and processes. In the past, many organizations have successfully saved financially by leveraging their own technology teams for new technologies. These organizations have benefited from internal staff providing stronger customer service than was available from the market. The future is *cloud*. The future is SASE. The future is *managed*.

In the next section, we will discuss the co-management model of SASE.

SASE Co-managed

Co-management, or *cooperative management,* is an agreement to share management responsibilities between two or more parties. This concept works well in arrangements where there is a clear delineation of responsibilities with discrete control mechanisms for each party to control their assigned area of management. An example of positive delineation of management or control is in cloud computing, where the **Cloud Service Provider** (**CSP**) is responsible for all platform operational activities, and the subscriber or tenant is in control of any service or application operating on top of that platform. In the CSP and subscriber relationship, there are clear boundaries with clear expectations from both parties.

With SASE, SD-WAN, security solutions, and related technologies, the lines of delineation seem to blur, as the management and control plane functions are designed for a single management operator. Often, due to the skills required for a successful operation of innovative and secure communications products, the customer or subscriber would like to leverage a **Managed Services Provider** (**MSP**) for the design, build, and deploy portions of the implementation project. The subscriber would like to have the ability to make changes on demand with support from the MSP as needed. This model of co-management, while beneficial for the subscriber in an emergency, is ineffective for service-level agreements for both the MSP and the **User Experience** (**UX**).

Slight changes pushed from the management plane to the control plane may create catastrophic effects on both security and data communications. All changes in a SASE or SD-WAN service require input from an experienced architect. The change control process for these types of sensitive and dynamic services must include an architectural review. In the past, most network or security changes impacted a single site and were easily correctable. As more automation is included in the software, the changes made to configuration tend to propagate through the service, which may cause undesired effects. These modern services will try to heal themselves at the expense of the UX. The speed of change, the automation of operations, the application sensitivity, and effective security benefits become a double-edged sword that cuts both ways. To effectively operate SASE, SD-WAN, or advanced security solutions, the staff must be trained to levels of expertise that have not been previously required.

To conclude, the co-management of many current technologies, including SASE, is highly ineffective due to the integrated nature of service policies. A minor change in policy may cause a ripple effect throughout the network, creating outages and security vulnerabilities. Effective secure communications require new levels of expertise that are not cost-effective for more than 90% of all organizations. The modern CIO is evaluated primarily on user experience and business value, neither of which is achieved by spending a sizable portion of the technology budget on training teams to operate ever-evolving secure infrastructure solutions.

In the next section, we will review the managed SASE service model benefits.

SASE Managed

Effective management from a SASE perspective will be contractual. The modern IT organization must become effective at vendor management in real time. In the past, contracting was more of a procurement or legal team function. As we move into the cloud-native world, the average life cycle of an individual application running on a system is close to five minutes. In the past, an IT organization would spend more than a year evaluating applications, more than a year deploying those applications, and would plan to operate those applications for 10 years or more.

Today, the nature of DevOps allows us to create applications that are dynamically generated, both on-demand and provided just-in-time to meet the need. The speed of change will only accelerate in the future as we leverage resources where they are needed, when they are needed, how they are needed, and most importantly, providing the specific UX that is needed. By tearing down an application when it is no longer needed, the same physical system resources may be leveraged continually without the need for constant physical construction or deployment.

Secure communications infrastructure must keep up with the pace of the application world as it exists as virtual plumbing to provide a safe and clean water source to those that need it. For the on-demand variable, it is no longer viable to spend years getting to an effective solution. For secure communications solutions, the application is the payload and the reason for existence. The modern IT organization must focus on meeting the demand on time with the correct UX or be outsourced entirely. To maintain pace, the IT procurement process must be a subscription model that allows for flexible consumption of services. The acquisition of flexible resources through subscriber models will provide the structure necessary to respond on demand to end user needs.

A dynamic cost management platform is needed to manage **Service-Level Agreement (SLA)** requirements, align the UX on demand, and support the lowest possible cost consumption model, while delivering on the required performance and productivity. Automating cost controls allows the services contracted to reclaim, reuse, and tear down after the expiration of the application or even the platform benefit. Automating the SLA and dynamically tuning consumption models to meet the internally required UX on-demand supports the required organizational performance the IT department was hired for.

The MSP can hire enough talent, divide their areas of specialization into **Centers of Excellence (COE)**, rotate the team through continual levels of training, invest in AIOps, invest in performance tuning AIOps, and leverage economies of scale. The COE function allows for a small team of continual learners to stay ahead of the next software release with every SASE service released by each manufacturer. The COE then trains teams just-in-time with the software release to be able to take advantage of positive changes in the software, as well as prepare for negative changes that may cause incident tickets to flow in.

Currently, the effective management of SASE, SD-WAN, or security in general requires effective AIOps to eliminate false positives, automate ticket correlation, resolve repetitive issues, maintain quality control, respond in real time to SLA impacts, trigger orchestrated solutions, and maintain quality scoring systems. AIOps will progressively automate the resolution of every ticket, with a strong focus on resolving security incidents. The financial investment in effective AIOps for security systems is a viable option at the scale of an MSP or a CSP, but not cost-effective for more than 90% of organizations.

The MSP's primary focus is secure communications at scale, while the end user organization is challenged with ROI on investments in the resources to effectively address the constantly changing nature of the **SASE Services Framework**. To be effective with the latest market solutions, the skills must be built into the team. Often, organizations falsely assume the market offers many options to hire the right person or team. Unfortunately, the last 5 years in the market have taught us that the right skills are non-existent in the open market. Examples of the skills required evolve every product sprint cycle due to the evolution of the software itself. Previously, hiring college-trained, manufacturer-certified persons with sufficient industry experience worked. This is because the products were being released in three to five year cycles with the next generation of hardware. In the software-defined world, the product evolves multiple times during the hardware's production life cycle. This forces the needs of the market to outpace previous educational efforts.

The pace of innovation has consistently shown that great products and services have launched on the market with fewer than 100 qualified persons globally. In the past, products we developed and launched in the 3- to 10-year range allowed for IT staff members to become aware of the need to study the changes prior to proof-of-concept studies. Today, the study material does not exist until the product is fully launched and the early adopters are actively in production.

To further underscore the gap in available educational resources, at the time of authoring this book, there are only two published books on SASE. For your convenience, both are listed here and offer great technical details for engineering teams. Please note that this is more than a year after my team installed SASE services for customers. The industry standards for SASE are still in draft mode and may not be published for another year. These are the two published books:

- *Journey into the World of SASE,* by Rohan Naggi and Ferdinand Sales, VMware Press, April 2021, ISBN-13: 979-8744750435.
- *Secure Access Service Edge – A Complete Guide* – 2021 Kindle Edition, by Gerardus Blokdyk, October 13, 2020, 5STARCooks.

To sum up, leveraging SASE with the pace of the market requires an innovative approach to education, expertise, skills, labor, management, contracting, and operations. The effective organization must spend more than 80% of its focus on its primary objective or revenue source. If your organization is earning its revenue through DevSecOps for secure communications infrastructure software, it will be significantly more cost-effective to outsource to a managed services provider than to build your own everything.

In the next section, we discuss the operational requirements for successful SASE services.

SASE Operational

The **operational** environment standards for SASE are exacting. The standards must be set, refined, optimized, reviewed, reported on, and continually elevated to achieve the minimum standard for a positive UX.

In military *special operations*, the term *operate* can be considered a noun, a verb, an adjective, an expletive, a motto, and a way of life. *Special operators*, as they choose to call themselves, operate on a different level from their conventional military force counterparts. While the military holistically operates in a manner that honors the tradition of those who served before them by changing slowly over time, the special operations community redefines their skills and operational models as often as every time they perform a new mission. *Resting on your laurels* is a concept that does not have a place in the ethos of any of the world's special operations units, and neither should it fit within your organization.

Taking time to celebrate a job well done provides strong psychological benefits for all humans, and serves to promote performance culture. Falsely celebrating low standards of performance can have an equally opposite impact on culture. To achieve positive UX, a defined SLA is required both internally and externally to the end user organization. To consistently achieve positive UX, automations in the *tools of the trade* are required.

To effectively operate SASE, ideally, the network and security operations teams would be combined and cross-trained. In the SASE world, the policy is the law, and only those who understand the law should participate in legal debate or, in this case, secure communications policy standards. SASE is policy-driven in the same way that a courtroom is driven by the letter of the law. The security operators are used for policies blocking or mitigating undesired network communications traffic. The network operators are used for policies that are forwarding, shaping, and providing quality to network communications traffic. As said earlier, in the SASE world, the policy is the law, and combines both network and security functions. With SASE, a mistake in policy not only causes undesirable effects on forwarding and blocking behavior at a single site, but it also replicates globally in a catastrophic chain of events. Effective SASE policies require effective operational strategies.

Effective SASE operations require effective toolsets, such as the following list. The list of tools is meant to be an example and is purposely not exhaustive. The nature of SASE is that for every year this book is in production, dozens of new tools will be created. The importance of the list is to create a starting point for an organization to create its own framework for operating SASE.

The *tools of the trade* sampling list is as follows:

- **Master Orchestration Platform** – This will be the **Multi-Domain Service Orchestrator** (**MSDO**) that maintains a push/pull relationship with individual service or product orchestrators.

- **Network Management System** (**NMS**) – This is typically what an SD-WAN vendor calls their orchestrator. The value of the SD-WAN orchestrator or the firewall management platform is specific control of that element of the overall solution. This can collaborate intraoperatively with the master orchestration platform.

- **API Manager** – Almost every software-based product today has an **Application Programming Interface** (**API**) library available for rapid integration. To effectively scale automations and integrations, a management platform is required to function as a spine to maintain structure for the individual API for each function integrated. This approach allows the genius of DevOps methods to be leveraged in a modular fashion as opposed to the legacy linear fashion. Modules may be easily substituted where the linear development's foundation is damaged each time a component is changed.

- **Service Management Platform** – All SASE service feedback needs to be evaluated for potential incidents or problems in the environment. The ticketing system can no longer be a standalone operations management platform. The service management system must be embedded into the solutions architecture as operations are a key component of DevOps. Integrating via API and collecting logging at all levels, collecting quality measurement data, collecting reporting information, collecting SLA measurement data, integrating architectural design knowledge, and any other feedback into a central location is key to all operational decisions. Central management of all known information about the SASE service is a prerequisite for effective automation and AIOps.

- **AIOps Platform** – The branded solution that is chosen will have a management tool for operating the AIOps individual service components. AIOps will combine all available data as well as machine training models to dynamically learn from gaps or failures. The expectation for effective AIOps is that in the first year, 90% or more of incidents are discovered, logged, and resolved without human interaction. First-year expectations for problems, recurring incidents, and resolutions should be in the 50% range. Each percentage point of progress in both *incident* and *problem resolution* should be celebrated, as significant labor investment is required on the path to 99.999%, which should be the goal of every organization. The changing nature of business and secure communications makes 100% a financially irresponsible goal.
- **Service-level Management** – The tool for managing SLAs is necessary as it provides the standard by which effective service operations are measured. Without this tool, success is subjective and will cause excessive financial consumption of services.
- **Cloud Cost Management** – The subscription model creates the agility for organizations to develop, deploy, and operate software-based solutions in a near to real-time fashion. Unfortunately, everything has a cost, and the pursuit of business value can be zealous. Well-meaning organizations, trying to achieve the performance level demanded by their end users, are subject to excessive resource sprawl and excessive resource consumption, which drives cost. Deploying an effective cost management solution allows for real-time cost feedback that may balance with the SLA.

In conclusion, to be an effective operator, you must have the right tools and the right training, both of which must evolve based on the mission dynamics. In the next section, we will focus on SASE success.

SASE Success

What does it mean to achieve SASE success? Just like every question in life, the answer is, *it depends*. Funny does not come close to describing the humor factor or the level of quantum computing required to answer the question on a technology framework that is evolving iteratively in real time with every developer releasing new software every week.

Success. From the *Merriam-Webster.com* dictionary, Merriam-Webster, as found at the following link: `https://www.merriam-webster.com/dictionary/success`. Accessed December 1, 2021. *Essential meaning of success:*

1. *The fact of getting or achieving wealth, respect, or fame*
2. *The correct or desired result of an attempt*
3. *Someone or something that is successful: a person or thing that succeeds*

SASE Success may be defined as a combination of all three listed dictionary definitions, as explained in the following:

1. SASE success should not hinder the organization financially from achieving its goals.
2. SASE success should be delivered correctly, not only for the emotional and financial wellbeing of the team or organization, but to protect and support the organization.
3. SASE success is the result of both individual contributor and organizational achievement in the form of safe, secure communications.

SASE success is not the deployment of a static product offering the way any other product has been delivered by your team. It is not a one-time project nor a product that solves all problems.

For success, the idea of SASE must be approached from an entirely fresh perspective, whereby each service built into the SASE framework must complement and support all other services in the framework. The project is never actually complete, as DevOps methodologies offer a CI/CD approach and, therefore, SASE must be an ongoing improvement program. The program management should be rotated as often as every three sprint cycles to enforce the idea that SASE teams may not rest on their laurels.

Overall, SASE success, while a subjective idea, is the idea that successful SASE will only be achieved in motion and never at rest.

Summary

In this chapter, we covered the management models for SASE, which include self-management, co-management, management by the service provider, operational management, and SASE success. The benefits of SASE are achieved through the effective management of an ever-changing framework of services for secure communications. SASE introduces the idea of aligning skills at the pace of DevOps methodology. Often, an organization must sacrifice ideal goals to align with the organization's primary purpose. This primary purpose is not always the most effective security or network infrastructure software development organization in the world.

Unfortunately, the organization's purpose, budget, acceptable risk, and culture make self-management of new generations of software a cost-ineffective goal. Outsourcing with effective vendor management becomes the most cost-effective means of conducting business. SASE success depends on individual and organizational evolution.

In the next chapter, *Chapter 4, SASE Orchestration*, we will be explaining what a SASE orchestration model looks like with sections on *Manual integration, Template based design, Integrate via API, Orchestrate to scale, and Automate to benefit*. By leveraging orchestration, the SASE framework becomes something that can be easily managed and scaled to any size without increasing labor requirements significantly.

4
SASE Orchestration

Scale is never achieved in a linear fashion as labor is never available at the rate of organizational growth. For an organization to scale at the pace of its growth, a non-linear or modular process is required. A successful process will require an understanding of architecture at both ten and one hundred times the currently needed sizing. Once the theoretical worst-case scenario is documented, the question of *how* must be asked. Assuming labor is static, how would it be possible to scale one hundred times the current size of the architecture? With human labor, it would be statistically impossible; therefore, non-human labor must be employed. Currently, the most effective way to scale infrastructure, virtual machines, or applications is to leverage an orchestrated model as well as an effective orchestrator. That orchestrator requires tools that abstract the process into modular components that are pre-built and made available on-demand.

In this chapter, we will discuss the downside to the manual operation of SASE, the benefit of templates, effective API integration, how to orchestrate SASE in an effective-to-scale model, and the benefits of automation.

We're going to cover the following main topics in this chapter:

- SASE Manual – understanding the scope of the manual operation of SASE
- SASE Template – understanding a templated model and its use
- SASE Integrate – understanding the basic API integration purpose
- SASE Orchestrate – understanding the basics of orchestration
- SASE Automate – understanding the benefits of automation

SASE Manual

The manual method of managing SASE, while simple and easy for seasoned operational teams, varies greatly between each service integrated into an overall SASE framework-based solution. A single organization may have dozens of SASE services, all of which have their own management platform. Each service requires the continual focus of the operational team to maintain security, quality, and performance requirements. Each individual service will require training. Each service will require a different configuration set. Extensive cross-service testing will need to be performed in a lab prior to exposing it to an end user. Each change is an opportunity for a lapse in an SLA. Each change will affect the end user experience.

The value of every device, logical service, application, or platform being operated by a one-on-one human for support evaporated more than 20 years ago. Many years ago, a major corporation would custom-build desks individually for management employees at the time they were promoted into their management role. Today, gone are the corporate craftsman, gone are the elevator operators, gone are the bathroom attendants, gone are the switchboard operators, and gone are many other roles where we valued their level of professional perfection.

Today, we must accept that the manual operation of technical service platforms is a disservice to our employer. We must accept that for every organization that requires 180 days to deliver a new service to their customer, there is a start up organization doing the same work through automation in 180 seconds. The market has spoken. It determined in the 1980–1990 decade that a cost-effective solution at 85% of perfection is the standard. While many organizations will pay a premium for solutions that are much closer to perfect, the consistent seller is the solution that is *good enough* for consumption. Since that decade, most of the companies that failed to listen to their customers' communication through actual purchases have failed. Many of the greatest brands prior to the 85% era closed through financial insolvency or had to sell their business to competitors.

Understanding that cost-effectiveness is valued over perfection allows leaders to look for solutions that allow their labor to evolve in a qualitative versus quantitative fashion. By improving the skills of a team, the headcount can remain static or decline while the quality of the services continues to improve. This concept is the predominant reason for business leaders improving value while reducing costs.

Concluding the discussion about manually operating SASE, the manual operation of complex software-based services is financially irresponsible. An effective fiduciary will invest in automation for every responsibility they have within the organization. An effective organization will focus on the education of its operations team and will incentivize each iteration of effective automation that improves user experience.

In the next section, we will discuss templating for success.

SASE Template

The templating process provides a method for seeking common ground in any technical architecture. From the simple template that a carpenter makes to repeat a design for a wooden chair to the complex templates used by **Cloud Service Providers** (**CSP**) to provision services on-demand, templates are used everywhere for consistent results. With SASE, SD-WAN, or cloud-based solutions, the use of a template is a requirement for scale, performance, consistency, and security.

In this context, a template is just a software-based, repeatable model that is created during the design process. This template is to be leveraged on demand for standing new services up. By templating the design of a site, service, device, connection, policy, or another solution component, each subcomponent of an approved architecture becomes consistent. Through consistency, scale is an available option, whereas legacy models that implement one subcomponent at a time with human labor create a variation that affects reliability and security.

Imagine the corporate acquisition of a competitor that has 1,000 locations, 6 data centers, and 25 cloud instances. The combined physical, virtual, and cloud services are supporting 500 separate applications with close to 10,000 virtual machines. Due to contractual and regulatory obligations, the assumption of technical management services must be completed within 24 hours. This assumption includes converting from MPLS to SD-WAN, installing new hardware, connectivity, security, and a SASE framework. It includes moving every service, application, compute system, and physical asset out of the data centers. The acquiring team must discover, migrate services, and vacate every cloud instance. Every virtual machine must be replicated into a micro-segmented, secure environment that did not exist prior to acquisition. What technology team can perform everything required within 24 hours to meet requirements that vacate liability for non-performance on a contract? Impossible is just an educational gap in this situation. It is currently possible with 21 days or fewer of planning to achieve a 24-hour conversion at this complexity level and which is repeatable.

Not only is it possible to implement a solution such as the one described here with hundreds of thousands of variables within 24 hours, but also the technology has been available for several years. The solution is the template. By creating a library of templates, an organization can instantiate almost any new service within an hour. The new service may take an hour in the provisioning process with timing depending on the system restart process. The timing assumption is that the average virtual machine can take up to 20 minutes. To apply configuration templates to the virtual machines, depending on the tool or process, it may take up to three restarts to accomplish production requirements for the new system. Many of the services used today across cloud-native or container systems have quicker cycle times, which may bring service instantiation down to less than 1 minute. In project planning, it is important to allow time for validation prior to production, which drives quality to insist on timing that would be more than 1 hour prior to the first time any service is offered in production.

The template leverages all lessons learned in previous attempts, both successful and unsuccessful. Often, the unsuccessful attempt serves as the best tool for education. Each attempt creates the opportunity to solve requirements faster. The race car pit crew provides an extremely useful analogy in how it takes multiple services that would each require a full day at an automobile dealership and performs those services in two to three seconds. The problem and the solution are both human. The educational process must combine the best of academic and vocational thinking while setting new standards for achievement.

In summary, the template serves as a pre-built, validated, repeatable tool for consolidating complex design efforts into a copy and paste function.

In the next section, we will discuss integration by leveraging an **Application Programming Interface** (**API**).

SASE Integrate

An API allows for custom, on-demand service integration. Leveraging an API allows multiple systems to interoperate with minimal effort and produce compounded benefits. Almost every software service on the market today allows integration via an API. An API can map functions between two products whereby a push and pull relationship is created. If we think of each separate SASE service as a module, an API connects the modules while defining the correct relationship via policy.

The future of all software-based solutions requires a data interchange through a common API framework. This framework operates as a spine of sorts, providing structure and commonality between services. Each module can be visualized as connected to the spine through a rib that is the API. Today, this is not a common approach, as most organizations are using a series of APIs in an as-needed fashion. The issue with the as-needed approach is that it requires a defined project to custom solutions for an organization's needs. By standing up the framework approach, it stays in production as a common approach, and only a provisioning team with a new service is required for success. This is achieved by the framework being stood up with common standards with the spine as the A end and the new service, the rib, as the Z end. The new service simply leverages published standards for connections that continually stand in production.

A common framework for an API will require an API management platform that enforces compliance with policy, enables security audits, and provides telemetry data to both **Security Information and Event Management** (**SIEM**) and service management platforms.

Ultimately, an API provides the much-needed feedback systems required for successful AIOps. The API integrates services into a solution with minimal DevOps investments.

In the next section, the orchestrator puts everything together to trigger success.

SASE Orchestrate

The orchestrator can be a tool, platform, service component, management system, or service provided to direct intended actions from software-based services. Generally, the orchestrator refers to a software platform with a suite of tools that manage, operate, configure, monitor, enforce policy, and perform many other necessary functions at the management plane in a software-defined network.

"Orchestrator (Concert and Stage): An orchestrator takes a composer's musical sketch and turns it into a score for orchestra, ensemble, or choral group, assigning the instruments and voices according to the composer's intentions." (`https://www.berklee.edu/careers/roles/orchestrator`).

Much like its musical equivalent, the orchestrator is balancing the collaborative participation of all the individual subcomponents of a solution. These subcomponents can be a configuration file, a software image, a network services template, a virtual machine, a set of policies, a cloud service, a physical device, and other necessary solution subcomponents. The orchestrator can even initiate the human logistical processes of designing, building, deploying, shipping, receiving, installing, testing, reporting, acceptance for change control, and optimization of all people and machine processes.

The orchestration platform directs every component in the overall solution to create the desired outcome. The parallel instantiation of millions of service components becomes possible by the orchestrator queuing the instantiation of services that are previously templated. The orchestrator interacts with each modular subcomponent in pretty much the same way the human equivalent would. Previously, large-scale software changes were performed by a triggered script-based process. The script would execute changes that expected every instance of the target software to be identical. This expectation proved to be unrealistic, as 97% of large-scale, scripted deployments would fail. The script-based process lacked the intelligence to handle nuance. The orchestrated model, when implemented correctly, treats each target independently, taking specific feedback from the target and adjusting the approach to ensure success.

The key benefits of orchestrated modes are as follows:

- Push-button, rapid-service instantiation
- Forced service template compliance for performance and security
- Telemetry collection from physical and virtual solution components
- Integration with automated service platforms
- AIOps integration for rapid healing

The **Multi-Domain Service Orchestrator** (**MDSO**) provides the ability to operate subordinate orchestrators and management platforms via an API. An environment that grows to multiple orchestration platforms needs a master orchestrator, which can be any available platform but must have authoritative control over its subordinates. This consolidation of control in a hierarchical model allows for common telemetry as well as the grouping of tasks that must be performed. Integrating two orchestrators equally can cause rework, as each will have the ability to trigger an opposite action to the primary action.

The master orchestrator, or single orchestration platform, must have integration with a **Network Management System** (**NMS**), an API Manager, a service management platform, an **Artificial intelligence Operations Platform** (**AIOPS**), service level management, and a cost management platform. Each integration allows the orchestrator to further reduce costs while enforcing compliance with the certified templates in production. The more integrations the orchestrator has, the more effective the orchestrated model becomes.

In short, the orchestrator provides the key functions required to reduce human labor while deploying solutions at any scale.

In the next section, we will focus on automating the SASE solution.

SASE Automate

Automation is simply the completion of work activities without dependency on human labor. Simple automation, such as a photocopy machine leverages, are triggered by human input. With the copy process, the activities performed by humans are placing the paper in the copy tray, selecting any desired settings, selecting the desired quantity, pushing the copy button, and retrieving the original along with the copies.

Complex automation still requires human input for success; however, tool systems such as AIOps can self-trigger activities to achieve specific outcomes based on policies designed by a human. With **Machine Learning** (**ML**), an AI-based platform can collect information from all available sources and run a training model to learn how to perform a specific task with desired outcomes. For instance, an organization wanting to automate service ticket resolution can train the AIOps solution to learn how to be a **Microsoft Certified Systems Engineer** (**MCSE**) as well as a **Cisco Certified Network Professional** (**CCNP**). The AI/ML solution learned to solve technical issues with both Microsoft and Cisco factory training models. This enabled the AIOps to successfully resolve tens of thousands of tickets by performing the work of an MCSE on servers and a CCNP on network devices. The initial training became 90% effective on first touch, ticket resolution of issues covered by MCSE and CCNP training. When the scope of the incident fell outside of the factory training model, the AI/ML was able to learn how to resolve issues it was not trained for by observing a human engineer resolve them. With the next matching incident, the AIOps virtual engineer was able to resolve it without human intervention. By leveraging this AIOps model, the platform was able to do the work of hundreds of engineers with the only limitations based on the available compute resources, software licensing, and the available training material.

The forward strategy for any organization should be to automate or outsource repeatable tasks, leveraging AIOps either directly or through a managed service provider. AIOps reduces waste, speeds up service resolution, improves the SLA, improves the end user experience, and returns labor to the host organization.

In conclusion, automation brings a larger return on investment than almost any other technical investment when implemented correctly.

Summary

In this chapter, we covered the downside to the manual operation of SASE, the benefit of templates, effective API integration, how to orchestrate SASE in an effective to-scale model, and the benefits of automation.

By orchestrating and automating the SASE solution, we reduce the educational requirements required to operate and scale SASE. The acceleration of complex technical solutions will not slow down in the future. As technology leaders, we must leverage the disaggregation of solution components to create a modular service substitution approach. This method of breaking down the solution into smaller pieces and applying strict orchestration policies makes the whole solution easier for the AIOps platform to operate.

In the next chapter, *Chapter 5, SASE SD-WAN*, we will be detailing the relationship between SD-WAN and SASE with sections on the *SD-What, SD-Why, SD-How, SD-When,* and *SD-SASE* that speaks to the effective integrated solution.

5
SASE SD-WAN

Secure Access Service Edge (**SASE**) and **SD-WAN** are two technologies that appear similar on the surface and may seem to overlap in the market. It is possible to buy either solution separately, successfully operating one service or the other. However, for secure network communications, almost every organization will operate both SD-WAN and SASE as an integrated and interdependent secure platform.

In this chapter, we will provide an understanding of what SD-WAN is, why to use SD-WAN, how to use SD-WAN, when to use SD-WAN, and what SD-WAN looks like when integrated with SASE.

We will cover the following topics in this chapter:

- SD-What – understand what SD-WAN is
- SD-Why – understand why to use SD-WAN
- SD-How – understand how to use SD-WAN
- SD-When – understand when to use SD-WAN
- SD-SASE – understand what SD-WAN integrated with SASE looks like

SD-What

SD-WAN stands for **Software-Defined Wide Area Network**. The SD-WAN replaces the routed WAN with a software-defined network solution. Simply said, SD-WAN replaces routers with next-generation technology for secure, site-to-site network communications.

SD-WAN breaks down network communications into separate logical *planes* of function. This is a further abstraction from existing manufacturer data and control plane separation, which focuses more on the physical allocation of resources. The SD-WAN solution takes advantage of separate logical control and data planes to allow for the specialization of each solution component or module. A routing protocol forwards traffic with the data as a payload and the control function is embedded. SD-WAN functionality forwards data in a per-packet or per-flow steering direction given by the controller based on policy. This separation between planes allows for independence of operation, resilience in communications, rapid changes, real-time security, and the insertion of **Artificial Intelligence for IT Operations** or **Artificial Intelligence Operations Platform (AIOps)**.

Most SD-WAN solutions take advantage of multiple circuits and forward across all available paths with an aggregation-like functionality. The benefits of SD-WAN accelerate with two or more different circuits per site. It is common for organizations to leverage three to eight separate circuits at an important location across two SD-WAN devices in high availability or multiple devices in clustering configurations.

Software-Defined (SD) leaves open the possibility of any function imaginable by the software developer. The contrasting idea, which is the standard product, is hardware-defined. Physical components defined by an electrical engineering specification that forces the software to comply with physical feature sets are an example of hardware-defined products. Over the past one hundred years, almost every technology advancement was made with physical device improvements. Today, more than 90% of improvements are software-based improvements, a benchmark that will accelerate dramatically over the next 10 years.

Modern software-defined solutions operate from a policy standpoint, allowing changes in the virtual, physical-equivalent features to change on demand as quickly as code is developed to support the virtual feature. An example of this idea is the ability to leverage a device to change the port capacity from 10 Gbps to 40 Gbps on the Ethernet interface just by deploying a virtual upgrade. A similar upgrade process allows engines to have a virtual performance upgrade over the internet. An example use case is where a truck that was optimized for fuel economy at sea level must now haul a load over mountain roads that is 20% heavier, requiring adjustments for altitude and greater power for climbing. The owner could log in to the manufacturer's cloud platform and trigger the performance upgrade for a specific duration, or permanently.

Software definition is achieved with a template or overlay that, much like onion skin, overlays engineering drawings, takes a new configuration overlay, and places it over the old, creating the new running configuration. Much like the onion skin, the overlay can be removed as quickly as it was put into place. Most often, the overlay change process is effectively in place within one to three milliseconds. The overlay process allows for rapid change as well as failback when needed. The orchestrator pushes each overlay into place and provides instant feedback on positive and negative changes through visual analytics based on telemetry.

In summary, SD-WAN delivers much more value than the replacement of legacy hardware, software, and protocols. SD-WAN paves the way for secure, self-healing networks that can auto-provision and deliver significantly higher levels of quality than previous generations of routed WAN solutions.

In the following section, we will start to understand the why of SD-WAN.

SD-Why

The network, the internet, and the market are all evolving more quickly than technology departments can support. The old model is broken. In the old model, we upgrade hardware every five to seven years with many organizations running systems for up to 12 years. While this model is cost-effective from a capital expenditure perspective, it costs the organization the savings achieved multiple times over. The operating capital required for legacy hardware is put into labor, security mitigation, insurance, legal, lost productivity, organization performance issues, failed audits, and failed opportunities. The old model simply hides its costs and hurts the organization. Simply upgrading more quickly will not resolve the chasm between the old model and what is truly needed for success. Success requires a new model and a combination of technology, methods, tools, and education. The new model, when implemented correctly, can break even financially within 12 to 18 months while reducing long-term operational costs.

With software definition, virtual physical equivalency is achieved and may be surpassed through continual improvement. The use of **Common Off-The-Shelf** (**COTS**) hardware and a hypervisor or container system allows the software-defined solution to evolve at the pace of DevOps. Potentially, every six weeks a new generation of software-defined infrastructure products is released. Consider the firewall in production that needs real-time software updates to protect its organization from cyber threats. Imagine the base code is evolving a generational life cycle every 6 to 26 weeks depending on the manufacturer's DevOps cycles and a physical firewall will run out of physical system resources every 6 to 18 months. COTS hardware or cloud computes are leveraged as the primary points of installation for SASE services so that each service can acquire sufficient system resources to maintain a security posture.

Currently, purpose-built infrastructure hardware is purchased on a 5-year capital depreciation cycle, has a physical operation lifespan of 7 to 12 years, and will become obsolete within three years. In the next few years, purpose-built infrastructure is expected to reach obsolescence in 12 to 18 months from the purchase date. The average WAN, SD-WAN, security, cloud, or SASE project takes 36 months from start to finish. Looking at the math, something is wrong. There is no **Return on Investment** (**ROI**) or break-even analysis leveraging the old model.

Enter the new model. In the new model, a ubiquitous edge compute must be leveraged and connected to multiple **Cloud Service Providers** (**CSPs**). The hypervisor or container system used for the architecture should support service mesh architecture and should be common across all CSP platforms. This allows the organization to make everything SD. This allows the organization to use single-day software, hardware, SD-WAN, SASE, a firewall, security, the IoT, or any other technology installation. In this model, you can install as fast as the fastest parcel system can ship a device for physical installation. Once the base physical installation is in place, single-day, complex SD-WAN or SASE projects are the new normal. SD-WAN could be implemented at thousands of sites in 15 minutes. A new security function may be implemented in less than 15 milliseconds by leveraging the new model.

In summary, the why for SD-WAN is to allow a near real-time deployment of new releases or generations of secure SD-WAN solutions as they are developed. SD-WAN provides an organization the ability to focus on its mission instead of operating a WAN.

In the following section, we will discuss how to use SD-WAN.

SD-How

How to use SD-WAN is a common question today. SD-WAN should be used for most organizations as a site-to-site or site-to-cloud secure network communications platform, replacing routed wide-area-networks. SD-WAN should also be leveraged as the site-to-service connecting solution for SASE services. In the future, **Zero-Trust Framework (ZTF)** solutions will define the SD-WAN's role in the infrastructure solutions portfolio further, but at this time, SD-WAN simplifies access to SASE.

To leverage SD-WAN, all current network architecture should be simplified, removing policy-based routing or prescriptive configurations. An open architecture must be leveraged to gain value from the SD-WAN solution. Most of the best-engineered WAN architectures in production today must be stripped bare of what made them effective to prepare for SD-WAN and SASE. The 180-degree shift in design is due to the separation of control and data plane functions. The control plane needs the ability to respond in one to three milliseconds to policy-related, environment-related, performance-related, quality-related, security-related, bandwidth-related, or latency-related change, or any other change in the network.

For an organization to scale at the pace of its growth, a non-linear or modular process is required. The modular approach breaks complex processes into "bite-sized" pieces. Each piece or module is then easy to understand, becoming a simple task that any person or software may complete. Those modules may be completed independently of the project timeline, allowing a project team to complete tasks where they have all necessary resources without interdependencies.

Effective SD-WAN and SASE architecture has no resemblance to any prior generation of technology. The more design or configuration carried over from the legacy deployment, the worse the behavior of the new network becomes. Both SD-WAN- and SASE-based networks have a personality that was purposely missing from previous networks. That personality or secret sauce of the next generation of solutions is the precursor to fully autonomous, secure network communications.

Currently, the most effective way to scale infrastructure, virtual machines, or applications is to leverage an orchestrated model as well as an effective orchestrator. That orchestrator requires that we abstract the process into modular components that are pre-built and made available on-demand. The templates leverage these modules and the orchestrator triggers solution constructions from modules via templates.

At some point in the future, the digital identity of a person or machine will have a profile that is leveraged to create a fully isolated, microservices platform that will segment as well as associate on-demand services, security, and networks necessary for that unique identity's benefit. That future is possible in the next few years.

In the SASE bonus chapter of this book, an effective SD-WAN design strategy is covered in more detail.

In summary, SD-WAN is used when any site needs to connect to another site, cloud, or SASE service in place of legacy routing technology and devices.

In the following section, we will learn about when to use SD-WAN.

SD-When

The market believes that the key value of SD-WAN is the potential for cost savings of 50 to 90% compared to routed, legacy network services from telecommunications service providers. The time to use SD-WAN is anytime that managed network communications are not the core revenue source of the organization evaluating WAN solutions. SD-WAN offers superior resilience to network outages (blackouts) or network impedance (brownouts). SD-WAN offers superior quality mechanisms over policy-based routing. It also offers superior levels of security over routing and VPN-based solutions.

In the market, we have many sellers touting SD-WAN as a cure-all solution for network issues. Industry analysts believe that installing SD-WAN saves money. However, the technical debt from legacy solutions in production requires significant skill, time, changes, and financial resources to convert from a legacy WAN architecture to a SD architecture. The overhead from the redesign, education, and impact on the organization often consume the first three or more years of savings. The impact of increased outages (due to the cheaper circuit types leveraged to cause the savings) often cost the business several times the forecasted savings.

SD-WAN can significantly reduce the costs compared to legacy WAN hardware and circuits, but it requires new, different skills than those that almost all network engineers or network architects have. For this reason, more SD-WAN and SASE solutions are being outsourced to **Managed Services Providers** (**MSPs**). In the past, factory training programs produced significant quantities of skilled engineering resources. Today and into the future, the software development life cycles are accelerating new releases beyond the pace of training development. A new solution must be developed for just-in-time training. It may not be cost-effective in the future to solve for the pace required to train in alignment with software releases. AI-based solutions will leverage ML to learn and test the operation's functional roles at the pace of software development. This learning gap is widening, forcing the current solutions to AIOps instead of developing human talent as a solution.

Overall, SD-WAN is needed now to reduce the human cost of secure network communications.

In the following section, we will describe what SD-WAN integrated with SASE looks like.

SD-SASE

SD-WAN and SD-SASE are both based on the need for secure network communications. SD-WAN is an existing technology. SD-SASE is redundant nomenclature, as SASE solutions are expected to be SD. The reason for a SD-SASE chapter is to underscore the SD nature of future solutions. SASE is inherently SD on a per-service basis. Integrating SD-WAN with SASE leveraging SD tools and methodologies is the commonsense approach for the near future at least.

The simplistic view is that SD-WAN takes the place of the router at the edge of each network and then connects to other SD-WAN endpoints to securely forward traffic to where the necessary services exist. SASE industry standards incorporate SD-WAN into SASE services as a potential endpoint for secure communications to a physical or logical location.

Moving on to a security perspective, SD-WAN security mechanisms can securely interact with SASE services to increase the overall security posture of an organization. The ZTF and AI-based security operation solutions integrate to both maintain and dynamically increase active security with SD-WAN.

SD integration is performed commonly via API, may be templated, and should be orchestrated to achieve maximum cost and operational efficiency. The API allows rapid integration with increased controls over cross-platform functions. The template makes large-scale deployments possible. The orchestration platform as an enforcer ensures all deployments are compliant with the architectural and security requirements and stay compliant continually.

In conclusion, SD-WAN and SASE are companion solutions that should almost always be used together for any organization to effectively provide secure network communications.

Summary

In this chapter, we provided an understanding of what SD-WAN is, why to use SD-WAN, how to use SD-WAN, when to use SD-WAN, and what SD-WAN looks like when integrated with SASE.

SD-WAN and SASE, while not codependent, provide increased value when effectively integrated. An orchestrated SASE solution that leverages SD-WAN and is integrated via API, templated, and operated via AIOps reduces the human capital investment needed for long-term operational success.

All SD technologies are rapidly evolving at a pace that means that legacy technology department processes have become ineffective and must be redefined. Perhaps the human process for designing, building, deploying, integrating, securing, and operating future solutions should be SD.

In *Part 2* of this book, we will get more technical with the SASE technical perspective.

In the next chapter, *SASE Detail*, we will take a deep dive into what comprises the SASE Service, with these sections on the service: *Definition*, *Components*, *Roles*, *Requirements*, and Service in *Flight*. For technical readers, this section provides details on SASE services, as the standards are still being developed.

Part 2 – SASE Technical Perspective

Part 2 provides a detailed understanding of what SASE is from a technical perspective. This perspective provides an understanding of the technical evaluation or development of a SASE project.

In this section, there are the following chapters:

- *Chapter 6, SASE Detail*
- *Chapter 7, SASE Session*
- *Chapter 8, SASE Policy*
- *Chapter 9, SASE Identity*
- *Chapter 10, SASE Security*
- *Chapter 11, SASE Services*
- *Chapter 12, SASE Management*

6
SASE Detail

Currently and perpetually into the future, SASE is an evolving concept where its details are changing at the pace of market conditions. SASE was coined due to a pattern of consumption of security, network, and cloud services in the market. This combination of services provides improved quality, performance, and security. Security threats will force SASE to mature and then adjust to combat threats as they appear. The details around the SASE service are expected to evolve while improving the value proposition of the service.

Much of this chapter's resource material can be found in the SASE Services Definition (MEF W117) at www.MEF.net:

- SD-WAN Service Attributes & Service Framework (MEF 70 and MEF W70.1)
- Application Security for SD-WAN Services (MEF W88)
- Zero Trust Framework and Service Attributes (MEF W118)
- Universal SD-WAN Edge (MEF W119)
- Performance Monitoring and Service Readiness Testing for SD-WAN Services (MEF W105)
- MEF Services Model: Information Model for SD-WAN Services (MEF 82)
- LSO Legato Service Specification – SD-WAN (MEF W100)
- Intent-Based Orchestration (MEF W71)
- Policy-Driven Orchestration (MEF W95)

All MEF members can participate in SASE-related projects. Please connect with mef.net to learn more about how to become involved and/or join MEF.

In this chapter, we will learn about the SASE service, its working definition, components, roles, requirements, and service in flight.

We will be covering the following topics:

- Service Definition – correctly define what a SASE service is
- Service Components – identify the service's components
- Service Roles – identify the roles involved and their functionality
- Service Requirements – what is required for a SASE service?
- Service flight – what does the service look like while in flight

Service Definition

SASE is a secure communications service from the network edge to the cloud edge. It is integrated across all the layers of the service; the physical, data link, network, transport, session, presentation, and application layers, as defined by **Open Systems Interconnection (OSI)**. Previous generations of solutions addressed network connectivity at the network layer with some regard to data link layer requirements. Security generally focuses on either the application layer or the network layer, though many attempts have been made over the past 20 years to integrate the data link with the security model. SASE intends to ensure security across all the layers by starting with a **Zero-Trust Framework (ZTF)**. In *Chapter 16, SASE Trust*, ZTF will be explained further, but for now, we can explain it as follows: if security starts from a *deny all*, each and every layer must be validated before the next, security becomes pervasive in the service.

SASE does not create any of its services; instead, it operates as a mutual framework of services that can integrate policy-based service components. This integrated framework weaves a web of service interdependencies that systematically removes the security vulnerabilities while improving the quality and performance of the communications service.

Each separate SASE service must maintain an effective security posture for the overall service to be effective. There must be mechanisms to shunt or block services that fail to maintain integrity in the holistic service. Each service provider must be integrated dynamically so that there's a sub-millisecond response to solution integrity. This integration must be automated, it must be monitored by other services, and the other services must be able to isolate any integrity violations.

Secure AIOps must be considered as the pace of the issues in the modern world exceeds the pace of any human-based response. Each service has an independent control plane that could vary in terms of performance, which must be mitigated in real time. The value proposition regarding the level of training and skill that's required for the two to six-week generational product life cycle continues to promote the concept of *best-of-breed* services from multiple providers, with an overall managed services provider to integrate and operate the service. Many organizations have invested in a **Security Operations Center (SOC)** to see whether the threats outpace the capital that's available for investment. While it is key to have internal security talent, the software, system, and human resources that are required to combat the threat landscape become an excessive consumption of financial resources. Generally, such liability can be managed better by contracting with an organization that provides those services to thousands of customers. The solution is based on economies of scale whereas today, a single organization cannot meet cyber threats in a financially responsible manner.

In summary, a SASE service is a secure communications service.

In the next section, we will identify the service components of a SASE service.

Service Components

The components of a SASE service typically include **Identity and Access Management (IAM)**, an **Actor Access Connection (AAC)**, a **Policy Endpoint (PEP)**, and **Endpoint Connectivity (EPC)**.

IAM is a technology where someone or something's identity is validated before being granted access to a system. Once this has happened, the system or service that access has been requested for will be permitted or denied based on the access policy. The policy may restrict access based on the context surrounding the validated identity, such as the time of day, location, user role, application, IP address, or other known variables at the time of access. Access may also be restricted based on the access method or device. The IAM service may also terminate access based on input from another service, such as **Data Loss Prevention (DLP)** systems.

AAC is essentially the point where a person, device, or service is provided access to the SASE service. The **subject actor** is essentially the *A* end, while the **target actor** is the *Z* end for any new service that's initiated. The relationship between the subject actor and the target actor exists until the session is terminated. An example of this behavior is where an employee on a corporate network is accessing the payroll system from their computer workstation at a branch office. The payroll system is in the corporate data center at their headquarters office. The target actor is the employee, while the subject actor is the payroll application. Once the employee logs out, the session is terminated, and the relationship ceases to exist. The SASE service that's operating out of the ZTF must authenticate hundreds of reference points for the session to be established. The IAM service validates the user's identity and ensures they are allowed to access the payroll from the PEP.

PEP is essentially anywhere that policy is enforced. The policy must be enforced at every interaction. To access the payroll, the user must have logged into their workstation, which enforced policy from the network and system access service, which in many organizations today is Microsoft **Active Directory (AD)**. Before the request was sent to AD, the 802.1X solution allowed the workstation to access the network at the branch, which also served as a PEP and participated in ZTF. The SASE Edge device also participated in ZTF before connecting to both the LAN and SD-WAN services and serves as a PEP. The payroll application has similar dependencies to collaborate with ZTF, SASE, AD, 802.1X, and other services while performing as a PEP.

EPC, in most cases, will be provided by SD-WAN. Other services, such as routed WAN- or IPSEC-type network connections, will be incorporated into SASE. SD-WAN is the de facto standard due to the groundwork that's required for its integration. By starting with disaggregated control and data planes, the changes that are required for compliance with the policy are more cleanly implemented in real time. The EPC must be able to fully integrate with SASE services and must be based on a ZTF to be effective. Outside of this model, extensive labor is required to enforce compliance with the new policy while it's being developed. Inside this model, policy changes are delivered in a sub-millisecond, real-time model.

In summary, IAM, AAC, PEP, and EPC are the core service components of any SASE service.

In the next section, we will identify various SASE roles and their functionality.

Service Roles

Each SASE service component may perform one or more separate roles in the SASE service. In one case, the IAM service may serve as the authentication role, while in another, it may serve as the target actor to validate an access request. Each role that's performed must be validated when it's initiated. For example, in real estate transactions, an agent may be a buyer, seller, buyer agent, seller agent, third-party consultant, owner, lender, trustee, mentor, and so on. At the same time, the same real estate agent may be a combination of several roles. This is conceptually like the components in a SASE service as they can play multiple roles, with each role being governed by a separate policy.

A role, subject to change, affects access according to the policy that's being enforced. In one role, a user or system may have full access but have no access in a similar role. For instance, the automated maintenance request system on an office copier machine may need access to the internet to communicate a service request. However, the copier does not need to communicate with the fire suppression system within the building. The fire suppression system may need internet access, as per the local fire regulations, but is not designed to communicate with unrelated systems.

A role must also be logged for each session request. By logging each role, forensics may be conducted in real time. By leveraging AI operations, each role may be evaluated in real time for risk as it relates to the stale policy. The policy in question may either be logged for review or rewritten to preempt risk. The mitigation process would create a ticket for human intervention after preemptive action has been taken.

In summary, SASE service roles clarify a state of existence or purpose that may be leveraged for policy enforcement.

In the next section, we will identify what is required for a SASE service to function.

Service Requirements

The requirements for a SASE service start with secure communications and then improving on that concept. In terms of the requirements of the service, various business, performance, communication, and security needs must be met. From the perspective of the service itself, it will have requirements from the manufacturer, the industry, and the government. More information will be provided in this section.

Business requirements include cost, value, function, and ease of use. A well-designed solution will reduce current or future costs while enabling secure business communications.

Performance requirements include bandwidth, throughput, quality, latency, and the speed at which changes take place. The system should perform at the current market standards regarding performance and be able to adapt to increase performance as new performance resources become available.

Security requirements include encryption, encapsulation, logging, response, mitigation, remediation, and compliance. Currently, TLS 1.2 (RFC 5246) is the minimum acceptable standard for SASE. Leveraging a minimum in any standard category is not a strategic method to reduce the security vulnerabilities of any organization. Each standard will evolve, and the solution must outpace the threat.

Manufacturer requirements are those that are necessary to establish minimum viable services. Each software or hardware manufacturer will provide setup documentation on a minimum viable configuration for success. These requirements include power, connectivity, management, and multiple dependencies.

Industry requirements focus on safe interoperability in the market. The industry's perspective is to encourage cooperation but also demands that each organization's purpose is to *not harm* the industry. Effective secure communications systems exercise *good faith* efforts to reduce such risks for the industry.

Government requirements generally focus on importing, exporting, taxing, and compliance. The import and export functions for secure data communications intend to protect the market from inadvertently equipping bad actors with peer-level security technology. The taxing service provides financial resources for *state-sponsored* security efforts. Compliance requirements attempt to increase a cooperative security posture.

To summarize, the requirements are complex, have good intentions, are necessary, but should not be considered an effective security strategy by themselves. Keep in mind that bad actors can read every published security document. An effective strategy is to establish the minimum viable solution in a lab, test it, and then develop organizational-specific security that creates a multiplier effect over the minimums. This new strategy must not be published, must be automated, and must be actively audited for effectiveness in production.

In the next section, we will observe the service in flight.

Service Flight

An aircraft in flight is designed to embody the beauty of a bird in flight. The grace by which both birds (naturally) and aircraft (by way of technology) glide through the air has a freeing effect on the imagination. A SASE service in flight should have a similar flight effect to an aircraft but also incorporate how birds can fly without the need to use technology.

To set up the conditions for our flight, we will start in the desert with a single user and a single device that needs to access an emergency service. This device has power but no connectivity. To access the device, the user must authenticate locally on the device, so they will need an access code and a biometric identifier. Two methods become the entry level and a single method does not allow access. This can be secured by a third local identification method, but the fact that the user has the device also counts as a third identification component. At this point, the user has access to the device.

The next layer of security is that the local application must have **Multi-Factor Authentication (MFA)**. However, since there is no network communication at this point, the application rejects access and presents a request for internet or private network access to complete authentication.

Our user with access to a device in a desert can access the device but other than local files and utilities, the device offers no value. At this point, our user finds an oasis that happens to have a satellite-based router with public wireless access. The user repeats this process to access the mobile device, which prompts for network access once more. The user selects a wireless network that is being broadcast and is prompted for a name and an email address that can be validated for access. The guest access system responds with authorization for access and our user can reach the internet.

To make this possible, the wireless network had to authenticate through the satellite router to a service provider network and ultimately to the internet. The satellite router went through a similar process that the uplink and downlink satellite gateways did. The authentication servers for the satellite service had to authenticate. The **Secure Domain Name System (SDNS)** had to validate the IP addressing involved. In this short process, as few as two and as many as 100 different systems had to coordinate to authorize access for our desert user.

Now that our user has internet access on their device, they can launch the emergency service application through MFA. They have completed the three-step process for authentication, which means they can access the emergency service application. They can use the application to identify their location, which is now well known on the internet, and send a call for help, which is estimated to arrive in four hours. The application asks for permission to turn on the user's camera for medical evaluation, which also triggers privacy and health care requests for permissions. Our user gladly accepts all the system requests and is told how to hold the camera to get a scan of any affected area of their body, as well as how to take a picture for facial recognition so that they can match the user to any existing medical records.

The **Artificial Intelligence (AI)**-based system evaluates the user and notices dehydration, chapped lips, no injuries, fatigue, gender, height, weight, blood pressure, respiration, and other criteria for medical evaluation. The AI determines that the user can survive the 4-hour response time and recommends that they drink from the oasis and relax in the shade until help arrives. The AI also triggered a security system to evaluate for human, animal, or other environmental threats to life and determined that the oasis was safe for now. However, it did set a ticket to check automatically every 15 minutes by leveraging the camera and satellite images.

Each step of this process required multiple systems to communicate and cooperate securely. Many more steps are involved in this process that we haven't discussed, lending credence to the point that human intervention in the process cannot happen in real time. Any of these systems lacking effective security would be weak points that could have left the user in the desert to die as they failed or succumbed to both passive and active attacks.

In conclusion, SASE must be studied, designed, implemented, and operated effectively to provide value. The primary strategy must be to automate the implementation, integration, and operation of the SASE service.

Summary

In this chapter, we talked about the SASE service, its working definition, components, roles, and requirements, and then visualized the service in flight. A SASE service is simply a secure communications service. That service may be from a single branded software or hardware manufacturer or may be composed of multiple services from separate providers. The components of a SASE service include IAM, AAC, PEP, and EPC. This list of components will continue to evolve but this model helps us understand the various roles, which are subject to change each time a request for communication is initiated. Any endpoint can be in multiple roles at any given time, whereas each role requires separate security authentication and may be subject to multiple policies. The requirement for a SASE service is a least-privilege web of security policies and services. This web allows any service to restrict access, ensuring nothing slips through a gap. SASE services are complex, with constant updates that require automation for success. Effective security provides reliable access to any applications or resources that are necessary for the user to provide value to their organization or the world.

In the next chapter, *Chapter 7*, *SASE Session*, we will focus on connecting the target actor to the subject actor while discussing Session, UNI, Actors, Flow, and the Lifecycle. Each concept will be broken down to help you understand how a SASE session can be achieved and operated.

7
SASE Session

A **SASE Session** is the core function of any SASE solution. Connecting the target actor to the subject actor, regardless of the connection type, in a secure session, based on identity and context, is why SASE exists. The SASE session must be established correctly and any violations or gaps in the policy will prevent any new session from being established. Any violation of the policy, while a session is active, will result in the session being terminated. In the future, the life cycle session will police sessions in motion for active security, as well as heal session performance without terminating the session. At the time of writing, the **Zero Trust Framework** (**ZTF**) ensures no session is established if it doesn't meet all the criteria for secure communications. The **User Network Interface** (**UNI**) provides a service inspection and monitoring point, as well as various services. The SASE Application Flow Specification serves as an enhancement for understanding behavior on a per-application basis.

In this chapter, we will cover SASE Session, UNI, Actors, Flow, and the SASE Lifecycle Session. This chapter will be your key to delivering continually secure SASE services.

In this chapter, we will cover the following topics:

- SASE Session – what is an effective session
- SASE UNI – what is a UNI and is it required
- SASE Actors – what are the SASE actors and what are their functions
- SASE Flow - what is the flow of secure session establishment
- SASE Lifecycle - what is the lifecycle functionality of SASE

SASE Session

According to the MEF Forum, "*A SASE session, or session, is the ephemeral flow of IP packets between two actors.*"

The SASE session starts when one actor attempts to communicate across the network with another actor. Before establishing an active session, the authentication process must be completed. No data plane communications will occur without valid authentication to create a secure session.

The SASE **Managed Service Provider** (**MSP**) is responsible for managing the overall service to ensure no communications take place without all the security requirements being satisfied. When a secure session is established, the mission also includes quality monitoring to ensure all the communications meet the **Service-Level Agreements** (**SLAs**) that have been contracted for the subscriber.

In the process of building a session, the following steps occur:

1. The session receives a unique session ID
2. The session ID must be unique within the service
3. The SASE policy is applied to the session ID
4. Every actor in the session gets a unique ID
5. The actor ID gets associated with a provider ID
6. A session specification is developed to classify the session
7. Actor lists are created and maintained
8. Tables are built and maintained for session state tracking

Each step is necessary to break down the SASE session into smaller pieces that can be independently managed, validated, tracked, and leveraged for comprehensive service performance.

The SASE service must be secure from a ZTF perspective, must provide consistent performance, and must provide consistent quality.

Overall, the SASE service ensures that all the minor components are being independently managed correctly at their lowest level, which is compounded in the SASE session. This is further compounded into a SASE service that can then be combined with other SASE services for an overall SASE solution that meets the needs of the organization.

In the past, all the functions in a single, prescriptive WAN solution would have been scrutinized to try and achieve the perfect solution. Unfortunately, the more prescriptive a service implementation became, the more the configuration had to be adjusted to match the rate of changing conditions within the environment where the solution had been deployed. The solution could not evolve at the pace of change due to financial and human limitations. Moving to a disaggregated control plane model, we can leverage a policy to effect change at the speed of the operating environment's change. This policy defines standards of expectation, and the control plane interacts with the environment to effect changes that are within the expectation of the policy. For this reason, the policy should be written to provide as much control to the controller as possible and only prescript where necessary.

Successful security must be Zero Trust, but a successful network function is least prescriptive in a controller-based, software-defined solution set.

"A SASE Edge is a set of network functions (physical or virtual) that are located between the SASE UNI(s) and the underlay connectivity service UNI(s)."

– The MEF Forum

In summary, the SASE session is the heart of the SASE service. By breaking it down into its smallest parts, each part may act independently and the whole solution, when aggregated, becomes a living, breathing, effective solution.

In the next section, we will explain SASE UNIs.

SASE UNI

The **User Network Interface** (**UNI**) is where the service provider's network touches the customer's network. This is typically on the provider's router. With the SASE UNI, the touchpoint is per service and is generally a logical construct, though it might be a physical interface since the SASE UNI lies on another service, such as SD-WAN, and the underlay UNI may be provided via MPLS or another service for the physical touchpoint.

The underlay is the actual circuit from the service provider, such as MPLS, Switched Ethernet, LTE, 5G, or other circuit types. The UNI for the underlay is the handoff point from the **Provider Edge** (**PE**) to the **Customer Edge** (**CE**). This leverages the **Permanent Virtual Connection** (**PVC**), as established for the subscriber organization.

The SASE UNI is a logical point of demarcation from the overlay service, such as SD-WAN, when connecting to the customer's SASE Edge, which may be physical or virtual. The SASE UNI provides much the same value as the underlay UNI. Both serve as a monitoring point for SLA management by validating contracted service attributes such as uptime, errored seconds, quality, throughput, and other metrics. The SASE UNI generally uses multiple, diverse underlay platforms.

In summary, the UNI is the handoff point between the provider and the subscriber.

In the next section, we will discuss the actors in the SASE session.

SASE Actors

As per the MEF Forum, "*An actor is a user, device, or application that either wants to access another actor or allow themselves to be accessible.*"

Actors generally come in pairs in this generation of SASE services. In every SASE session, there is a subject actor and a target actor. The subject actor is at the "*A*" end of the relationship and does something based on the target actor at the "*Z*" end.

Regardless of their role, all actors are denied access using the ZTF until they are fully authenticated by leveraging a **Multi-Factor Authentication** (**MFA**) **Identity and Access Management** (**IAM**) system. IAM leverages factors such as risk, reputation, role, privilege, capability, and physical or virtual attributes such as a serial number or **Media Access Control** (**MAC**) address.

Once the actors have been authenticated, the subject actor and target actor for each SASE session are tracked, managed, monitored, and controlled so that they can be applied to that actor's SASE policy.

Identity is a known, fixed, constant attribute for a device, service, or user. The context in which a specific identity is accessing the service may be used as a condition for permitting access. The context of the authentication request may allow access. In the ZTF model for security, all access is denied by default and many conditions must be met to establish each new SASE session.

The following are some examples of context:

- Time of day/session start time
- Risk/trust assessment of the access device
- Presence (location, historical patterns, and so on)
- Authentication strength (weak, strong)
- Level of assurance (NIST levels, X.509 certificates)
- Risk assessment (pattern analysis)
- Federation (partner attributes)
- Device characteristics (fingerprint, device health, device protection, trusted data, and so on)
- Assertions from trusted partners (SAML tokens and more)
- **Single Sign-On (SSO)** sessions (session timeouts)
- Location, as defined by the SASE service, so that it matches the zones and policy (this applies to both target and subject actors)

In summary, SASE sessions begin and end with an actor in a role that may change per session. Each actor must be validated to retain access on a per-session basis; otherwise, the next session is never established. This is a major departure from earlier network communication systems. This departure is a ZTF foundational differentiator that is necessary for secure communications. Context acts as an added condition that allows access.

In the next section, we will follow the flow of secure session establishment.

SASE Flow

A SASE session flow is a decision-making matrix that allows packets to flow across the secure network connection in the SASE session. If an answer isn't provided for any of the interrogation process decisions, the packet is blocked and the session is ended. When the session is terminated, the authentication process is required for the next session, which ensures security measures are not violated.

MEF 70.1 defines an **Application Flow Specification** (**AFS**) as "*A named set of application flow criteria.*" The AFS is a key attribute for the SASE service to use in determining specific application behaviors. Via pre-identification, the SASE service creates an understanding of any predicted behavior that may be analyzed in flight to understand when non-predicted behavior occurs. Non-standard or non-predicted behavior triggers a security response to terminate bad actor communications. By terminating the session, good actor communication may reestablish communications through a new session, while bad actor communication will fail the reauthentication process.

Each SASE session may have multiple AFSs included in the session, but there must be at least one to establish the session. During the setup of the session, the AFS is compared to IP addressing as part of the validation process. When you're using SASE and SD-WAN, both the AFS and IP will be compared from both services to only establish the session when the common attributes are matched in both service policies. This is part of the least privilege model and supports both security and performance/quality goals.

To summarize, the flow of a SASE session is tied to the SASE session flow, which confirms communication pre-flight and monitors it for the intended behavior while in flight.

In the next section, we'll describe the life cycle functionality of SASE.

SASE Lifecycle

The SASE life cycle idea is one that Neil Danilowicz, while working on the MEF W117 project, came up with to allow AI-based security to be inserted into an active SASE session.

Once the SASE session is in place, the subject actor, the target actor, and the traffic flowing between them in the SASE session need to be monitored. This monitoring needs to be active to prevent security vulnerabilities and attacks.

SASE sessions are terminated as soon as the conditions in the subscriber policies are not being met. In other words, SASE sessions have life cycles that are orchestrated by the SASE service provider.

By creating a third wheel mechanism, a life cycle session can be established by leveraging the same security posture and session. This allows you to insert secure monitoring and management and prepares you for a future AI-based solution to actively mitigate quality, performance, and security that falls below the service levels defined in the SASE service.

In conclusion, the SASE life cycle session is a future-looking concept that will allow active, AI-based security to interact with an active session and dynamically fight cybersecurity threats in real time.

Summary

In this chapter, we looked at SASE sessions, alongside UNIs, actors, the session flow, and the SASE life cycle. The SASE Session is the lifeblood of the SASE Service; without it, no communications can take place in SASE. Many of the service components in the SASE Service exist to ensure no session is established without every individual component matching the requirements. In other words, each service component serves as a key to unlock another lock that prevents the service from working in a less than secure fashion. Once all the locks have been unlocked, the SASE Service functions as intended with great precision.

In the next chapter, *Chapter 8*, *SASE Policy*, we will explain the policy components of the SASE Service while covering SASE Policy, SASE Quality, SASE Dynamic, SASE Trust, and SASE Effective. The Policy is the key to all the factors in terms of security, quality, performance, resilience, path selection, and almost every control plane decision.

8
SASE Policy

SASE Policy defines every high-level function in SASE and most of its lower-level functions. It defines security in every sense of the word, as well as quality, performance, data flow, packet forwarding, traffic shaping, who, what, when, why, where, and how much for everything. With SASE, access to the network, access to the applications, and even access to devices are controlled with a policy. If a SASE Session is the heart of SASE, then SASE Policy may be identified as the lungs that breathe life into a SASE Service.

In this chapter, we will cover SASE Policy and discuss quality mechanisms, dynamic policy mechanisms, how trust is leveraged, and how to design an effective policy. SASE Policy can deliver exceptional quality and performance, or it can deliver more damage than anything else in the SASE framework.

In this chapter, we will cover the following topics:

- SASE Policy – explain what SASE Policy is and how it is different
- SASE Quality – explain the available quality mechanisms
- SASE Dynamic – explain the dynamic behavior driven by policy
- SASE Trust – explain the trust mechanisms and their functions
- SASE Effective – explain how to design an effective SASE Policy

SASE Policy

According to the MEF Forum, SASE Policy is defined as *"A policy that's assigned to a SASE Session that determines how a SASE Service handles IP packets in the SASE Session."*

It is a defined set of rules for governing action. The policy mechanisms of SASE are leveraged to enforce the desired effect. SASE Policy is essentially a composite collection of policies that are prioritized and start from a position of zero trust. If all communication is denied or blocked until it meets the minimum requirements for authentication and authorization, then the service can effectively support secure communications. Once all the security-focused policy's requirements have been met and the initiated communications session is allowed in the environment, then policies that forward and direct traffic can ensure that quality, path, performance, and other networking or applications policies are enforced.

At a high level, many SASE policies exist to collectively define all the operational details for a production SASE Service. There are a lot of policies available today and they will grow organically as new needs are identified. Each policy serves a role that would be less burdened if it was just part of a single policy and not separate, as identified here.

SASE policies currently include, but are not limited to, the following:

- SASE **Security Policy**, based on the **Zero Trust Framework** (**ZTF**), allows traffic to flow once authenticated and authorized.
- SASE **Security Functions Policy** is served within the security policy to block or allow traffic flows.
- SASE **Session Forwarding Policy** leverages the control plane to forward traffic on the best available path, as determined by quality and performance metrics.
- SASE **Subscriber Policy** allows the customer's intent to be made a reality by matching predetermined requirements for the SASE Session that are contracted and enforced.
- SASE **Policy End Point** is where the SASE policy is enforced.
- SASE **Notification Policy** provides notifications of events that may be informational or issues that require immediate action.
- SASE **Identity Policy** allows us to determine who or what is attempting to access the SASE Service.
- SASE **Actor Access Connection Policy** defines the conditions in which an actor is granted access and governs access throughout the session's lifetime.
- SASE **Context Policy** allows us to enforce a predetermined context for access to the service such as time of day, access method, day of the week, session duration, or location.
- SASE **Monitoring Policy** determines the scope of the monitoring services and the output from that monitoring activity.
- SASE **Composite Policy** is used to construct all the active policies in the SASE Service in order of priority.

The benefit of separating policies by functional area is like a sewing pattern made from translucent paper, with separate option components that can be added or removed from a garment's design. The model allows you to set out the base policy and then stack additional policies on top as needed to produce the desired effect. This overlay of multiple policies into a SASE Composite Policy allows complex designs to be built across a vast quantity of SASE endpoints in less than one percent of the time it would take to configure a policy on a firewall or router manually. The separation of policies has the added effect of allowing changes to be made across the globe in a few milliseconds as opposed to the hours that scripted changes or the weeks that manual changes would have taken. This is accomplished by making small changes to a single policy that, when saved, are immediately replicated. This change may be actively monitored, and then a rollback can be performed in the same few milliseconds if the change does not produce the desired effect.

Each independent policy should not overlap attributes with other policies in the same SASE Service. An overlapping policy allows independence in the hierarchical construction of the SASE Composite Policy. This allows policies to be leveraged on demand, triggered independently, or ignored based on the requirements.

The MEF 95 Policy-Driven Orchestration standard guides policy orchestration, which is key to scaling and accounting for policies. Much like its musical counterpart, the software orchestration platform allows the audience to feel the combined effect of many individual software policies performing their role superbly. The MEF Forum defines a policy as *"a set of rules that are used to manage and control how the state of one or more managed objects is changed and/or maintained."* An effective policy is strong enough to produce the desired effect but flexible enough to not produce undesired effects.

In summary, the SASE Session is the heart of the SASE Service and SASE Policy is its lungs. SASE Policy governs the rules of engagement for the SASE Service. Without effective policies, the service can't benefit its organization.

In the next section, we will look at the quality of a SASE Service.

SASE Quality

Quality in SASE is normally associated with the SD-WAN solution that's leveraged through the SASE Service. Network communications services generally associate quality with performance. In previous **Quality of Service (QOS)** models, a method of measurement for key attributes was employed and a configuration leveraged those measurements to enforce service-level standards. With SD-WAN quality mechanisms, many sophisticated tools may be used to measure quality. Then, the appropriate policy enforces **Service-Level Agreements (SLAs)** to ensure the service enforces quality control.

Performance measurements may include jitter, loss, latency, delay, errors, and **Mean Opinion Score (MOS)**. Going forward, SD-WAN solutions may include **User Experience (UX)** as part of their performance measurements. Many SD-WAN solutions have the raw ability to express UX through analytical data. In the future, quality throughout the SASE Lifecycle Session may also include active security engagement, whereby the session may be terminated, corrected, or healed by an active AI security operations model. Overall data throughput may also be analyzed for distributing sessions across many physical circuits, diversifying the workload for both performance and UX reasons.

In SASE, quality is applied to sessions through SASE Policy and may leverage all the performance measurement tools that are available to the overall service. Commonly, this quality will leverage the Monitoring Policies and be determined by Subscriber, Session Forwarding, and Actor Access Connection Policies. In some cases, the Context Policy may affect performance based on the context around the access. For instance, if the user is accessing an application from a location where the organization prefers to force traffic through additional security or an alternative geographical location, then a lower performance SLA may be acceptable to the organization.

The SASE Subscriber Policy is where the contractual enforcement of quality or performance per SLA should take place. The SASE Session Forwarding Policy should identify the underlay and overlay paths that are available. This should be related to application access and the current quality metrics and whether they identify the standards that have been met. SASE Actor Access Connection Policies provide layers 1, 2, and 3, as well as overlay assignments. SASE Monitoring Policies identify what is to be monitored, how it will be monitored, and how monitoring information is provided.

In summary, quality is measured, monitored, and enforced by SASE policy.

In the next section, we will look at dynamic policies.

SASE Dynamic

Prescriptive policies choke resiliency within the SASE Service and create work for operations teams and administrators. Service resiliency requires the ability to act based on real-time conditions or changes to the operating environment. A policy must provide options for the *secret sauce* of the service to restore secure communications as needed. In the past, policy-based routing was designed for perfect conditions.

When a less than perfect condition arose, such as a faulty circuit causing a *brownout*, where it would work intermittently but not effectively, the network operations team would have to troubleshoot the issue and find a solution. With most SD-WAN solutions, the service will move the session around the *brownout* circuit and trigger a notification. The notification may then be passed to the service management system, which then creates an incident in both the carrier's system and the host organization's system.

The system can be augmented with AIOps, where the ticket will follow the contracted escalation path until the service is restored. The SD-WAN software will automatically detect the *brownout* resolution and start forwarding traffic across that circuit again. Instead of hours or days of human labor, this entire cycle may take place over a few minutes or a few hours of machine labor.

Most of the SASE Services that are available in the market have dynamic healing algorithms for service components. The benefit of these dynamic solutions is hampered by the excessive design of SASE policies. Each policy in the SASE Service should be as least prescriptive as possible. The policies should not overlap. Each policy should be light, and success should be developed in the form of orchestration to leverage policies as needed. The overall SASE Service needs the least prescriptive model to pave the way for dynamic interaction with AIOps.

To conclude, SASE is dynamic and can be unnaturally restricted by excessive prescription in the policies. Keep the security at zero trust and the policy as open as possible.

In the next section, we will learn how to trust or to consistently not trust.

SASE Trust

SASE trust should always be zero trust. Many first-generation SASE offers have been based on SD-WAN or a firewall with added functions. The entire success of the SASE Service depends on effective security. For effective security, SASE deployments must leverage ZTF. SASE Security Policy will allow traffic that has met all the criteria for authorization; then, SASE Forwarding Policy will forward traffic as defined by that policy. **Identity and Access Management Function (IdAM or IAM)** serves as the basic building block for identifying who or what is trying to access the network. IdAM/IAMmay get you in, but ZTF will shut you down if something changes while traffic is in session. SASE trust is zero trust because there is never a time that a session should be allowed to exist unless all the policy conditions are continually met.

The first rule in SASE is that there is no trust. Any discussion about trusting in SASE should be considered using common vernacular and not considered to mean that any component, service, user, device, certificate, token, password, identity, or attribute is trusted.

To summarize, there is Zero Trust in SASE.

In the next section, we will learn how to make SASE an effective solution by using effective policies.

SASE Effective

An effective policy is a policy that meets the needs of the organization at the time it is implemented. Unlike a political or fiscal policy, SASE Policy must not trust – however, it must be fluid, dynamic, provide quality, and change as often as needed to continually be effective.

SASE Policy must take a layered approach that is prioritized from most critical to least critical. It must leverage a least prescriptive, open model that allows resilience in the architecture while it's being used. Conditions change, so the policy must adapt to allow for unplanned conditions.

To design an effective SASE policy, the basic layered approach to security must be used, starting with a closed ZTF-based solution and opening it when all the requirements have been met for secure communications.

In conclusion, an effective SASE policy allows secure communications services to be implemented if the security requirements are continually met.

Summary

In this chapter, we covered SASE Policy, SASE Quality, SASE Dynamic, SASE Trust, and SASE Effective as prime considerations beyond the branding of the SASE Service. Considerable costs, resources, labor, and time are invested in each SASE project. SASE provides a great solution for secure communications for any organization. SASE Policy is where the specific requirements for each organization will be met and delivered. It is where most of the skill and effort for any SASE project should be exercised.

In the next chapter, *SASE Identity*, we will discuss **Identity Access Management (IAM)** in terms of SASE, as well as Access Identity, Dimensional Identity, Context Identity, Situation Identity, and Integrate Identity. The who or what is key to secure access in a Zero Trust Framework that SASE must leverage for effective security.

9
SASE Identity

In a **Zero Trust Framework** (**ZTF**), no human or machine is allowed access to any resource until all the conditions of the policy have been met. Identity is a construct that establishes who or what is accessing the resource. More complex security mechanisms require a more aggressive approach to establishing the foundational identity of the who or what is requesting access to a specific resource. The evolving regulatory landscape requires not only validation before access but significant record-keeping to enable forensic research.

We must understand **Identity Access Management** (**IAM**) and **Multi-Factor Authentication** (**MFA**) before we can understand a ZTF.

In this chapter, we will cover SASE identity in terms of access, dimensions, context, situations, and integration. In addition, we will discuss how to integrate identity into SASE designs.

We will cover the following main topics in this chapter:

- Access Identity – describe Identity Access Management with SASE
- Dimensional Identity – understand multi-dimensional decision
- Context Identity – conceptually put identity into context for policy
- Situational Identity – explain situational identity models
- Integrating Identity – integrate IAM into SASE design

Access Identity

IAM allows you to validate who or what is accessing anything that's protected in the ZTF. Before accessing the ZTF, an identity must be established in a manner that's acceptable to the ZTF. MFA is often required to verify the identity of a SASE solution. At the time of writing, MFA is a required tool for almost every high-security standard, SASE Service, ZTF, VPN, and almost every compliance standard and government regulation. MFA is a prevalent requirement that should be considered the default requirement for all secure solutions.

The United States of America's **National Institute of Standards and Technology (NIST)** provides standard definitions of technology concepts and defines a common understanding of security concepts.

NIST provides eight separate definitions of identity. The intersecting thoughts for the concept of identity are unique, distinguishing, and recognizable attributes. Each separate definition tries to establish a mechanism where a standard can leverage something specific to isolate who or what is accessing a resource. This could be an application, system, network, dataset, or physical environment.

The most applicable definition for SASE comes from NIST SP 800-161: *"The set of attribute values (that is, characteristics) by which an entity is recognizable and that, within the scope of an identity manager's responsibility, is sufficient to distinguish that entity from any other entity."*

For further reading NIST identity topics, please review the following documents at `https://pages.nist.gov/800-63-3-Implementation-Resources/` or by searching at `https://www.nist.gov/`.

Document	Title
SP 800-63-3	Digital Identity Guidelines
SP 800-63A	Enrollment and Identity Proofing
SP 800-63B	Authentication and Lifecycle Management
SP 800-63C	Federation and Assertions

IAM is a systematic tool for maintaining identity data and is leveraged by other systems such as MFA. IAM is the overall administration tool for managing identity and can interconnect with other systems to enhance security. That is why it is commonly referred to as Identity Management or Identity Access Management. A framework for managing policies, identities, and resource access – IAM provides a holistic approach to managing identity.

A multidimensional approach is required to integrate IAM, context, situational components, time of day, location, and many other factors to deliver sub-millisecond, active security that is continuously relevant.

An example of IAM interacting with MFA is when a customer accesses their bank account through the internet. The banking system requires their user ID, password, and a security question through IAM. It is also important to note that the system tracks the device that's being used for access and may ask the customer if they want to save the device for future use. The system then triggers MFA by emailing or sending a one-time code that must be entered for access. Only after all the conditions have been met is access granted to the banking system.

The user identification and password method offers malicious entities access to a system often within 5 seconds. MFA solutions incorporate at least three categories or concepts – what you know, who you are, and what you have. The user ID and password may suffice for what you know with a **Personal Identification Number** (**PIN**) and additional security questions, thus adding complexity. The use of biological identification such as facial recognition, fingerprint, voice, retina, gait, or other unique human patterns adds a second dimension of complexity. Leveraging a secure token, certificate, badge, or specific device then adds another.

In SASE, to build on these MFA requirements, context and situation may be incorporated to add additional dimensions of complexity to help identify that the correct user or system has access to a resource.

In summary, identity defines the who or what is attempting to access a resource. The IAM and MFA solutions manage and verify that identity.

In the next section, we will explain multi-dimensional identity factors.

Dimensional Identity

The multi-dimensional security solutions provided by MFA allow the SASE solution to build a picture of who or what is accessing the system. This complexity allows the security system to maintain a digital identity for each user or device accessing the system. This identity becomes more complex each time the system is accessed, much in the same way as humans develop a more complex understanding of who a person is with each encounter.

This example shows the compounding nature of each interaction with a specific person you meet. Imagine meeting a person via a telephone call and then meeting them in person. Each encounter builds a more complex understanding of who that person is. Humans leverage every sense as well as every sentence to form what they consider to be that person's identity. If someone were to call us pretending to be someone who we had previously had multiple interactions with, we would feel that something is off. Each interaction drives the complexity of the identity construction we have for that person. The more we interact and the more ways we interact with that person, the harder it becomes for an impostor to achieve success.

The dimensional identity systems must mimic this human behavior and learn from each interaction to create a more complex understanding of either human or machine identities. This ensures that the imposter is immediately identified and denied access to the systems. In DevSecOps and AIOps, the AI must be able to build upon IAM to study the behavior.

Who, what, where, how, why, when, and how much are all dimensions that can be studied. These areas of study may be further compounded by biometrics, video analytics, certificates, tokens, access methods, devices utilized, behavior, policy, context, and situation. Each area may be compounded by leveraging an intersection of two or more areas of study. Today, this is essentially based on static policy, but the introduction of multiple AI-based solutions allows this security to become more dynamic. In the long term, the AIOps approach, when applied to security, will allow dynamic security solutions to be used immediately.

In summary, security has always required a layered approach to achieve success. The dimensional approach allows these layers to be compounded in effect.

In the next section, we will use identity in the context of a policy.

Context Identity

The idea of context is both easy and hard at the same time. In human interaction, context often eludes transference. The same sentence may be said in the same way and mean two different things, with the differentiator being the context where the same words are spoken. In some languages, context is constant but in most, context remains a variable concept. In terms of security, the same person may access a resource that is allowed in one context but denied in another.

For example, an employee may be allowed access to company banking software in the office but not from home. A laptop computer may be allowed to access any company system within one country but be restricted to specific systems when traveling outside that specific country. A user may be allowed to access the corporate network from the office they normally work at but not from an office within the company that has a higher or lower security policy. Some systems may be allowed during business hours and restricted outside of those hours.

In SASE, having an effective policy is relevant to the context that it applies to. An effective SASE policy is hierarchically layered and based on a ZTF. Ultimately, an effective policy will ensure no trust is established for access and each layer of the policy can unlock access at that specific layer. When an access request is made, each layer is only unlocked if the user or device meets the requirements for access at that layer. A simple user access request to check corporate emails may have to unlock 15 to 60 layers of the policy before access can be granted to the system. An effective solution will perform these actions in less than ten milliseconds and then remove any layer of access in less than one millisecond.

To conclude, context matters as the shift from being a positive actor to becoming a negative actor can be instantaneous. Context allows security to create differentiation to classify when the positive posture of an actor shifts to rogue.

In the next section, we will look at situational identity models.

Situation Identity

Identity in the context of a situation requires IAM that is capable of leveraging the situation as a policy component. Situational identity builds upon context to combine the static details with the immediate active environment. Without this layer, an active session may be maintained while an undesirable situation occurs.

During a change control event, a management session is desirable while an active user session isn't. In a commercial environment, electrical operations are necessary for systems that may be safety- or life-sustaining. In the same environment during a flood, such electrical systems pose a threat to human life. During a cyber-attack, allowing **Intrusion Prevention System** (**IPS**) to intervene at multiple levels, shunting system access, and potentially electrical systems, might be the best defensive mechanism.

AIOps allows situational awareness to be applied to context and leveraged in conjunction with other policies for dynamic intervention for negative situations. Leveraging an IPS solution to interact via an API with IAM and AIOps creates a complex construction of simple systems with simple policies that create a compound benefit for the organization.

Policies should always be simple and address as small a set of criteria as possible. Stacking policies in a hierarchical model provides a decision tree or matrix approach to *least privilege* security. The layered approach, when applied to external indicators such as situation and context, can address multiple dimensions and preserve the ZTF as needed to ensure overall security.

Prescriptive, linear policies create the opposite effect by trying to accommodate every eventuality, which is impossible. The prescriptive approach to security pre-dates the idea of a castle with a wall and a moat surrounding it as a secure fortress. Ingenuity, effort, and sometimes luck were able to defeat the moat, wall, and castle.

Modular approaches to security allow modules to be orchestrated to accommodate dynamic security interaction while data is *in-flight*. The model can be a singular policy or a single criterion for a policy that may be leveraged when the time is right, as part of a complex security system of modules that leverages simple policies in the right combination to achieve the desired effect.

Modular security systems are like children's building block systems, where different sizes and shapes interconnect with any of the other blocks from the same manufacturer. This system allows the child to pick any block that meets their desired goal in terms of color, shape, size, pattern, and so on. The magic to the child is that anything they envision or desire, they can build with the interlocking block system. We need to enable security teams to build policies in very much the same way.

To create a modular security system, each module must be inventoried and defined. With a specific SASE Service, this effort can be completed with configuration options. Creating a set of policies that are *least prescriptive* while leveraging as few of these options creates the basic policies that can be leveraged. A complete security policy will leverage several basic policies in layered combinations to create the desired effect.

To summarize, the situational identity changes based on the situation and must be accounted for in a complete security policy. The situation must also be accounted for to allow a user or device to retain an active session. Modular approaches to security allow a situation to be inserted into IPS, IAM, and The ZTF, allowing you to shut down active sessions that violate any portion of the overall security policy.

In the next section, we will learn how to integrate IAM into SASE design.

Integrate Identity

SASE provides direct integration paths and, in some cases, comes bundled with an identity management solution. Direct integration reduces the design, build, deploy, and operation cycles for the project but takes the disadvantaged approach of linear integration. In the early days of secure communications, linear integration was not just the only option for security but was a preferred quality mechanism.

Allowing a programmer to develop the security mechanisms from a foundational level up allowed the organization to achieve the desired effect with precision. This approach has been instrumental in academically training the critical thinking process that is espoused in college-educated engineering teams. In other words, the *right way* of developing products has been consistently proven wrong when measured financially, through performance-based metrics, tested for security, or audited for compliance.

Many organizations have failed financially in the past two decades by allowing linear software development. The Agile movement was created to combat this issue as the time to market for software was 3 to 10 years and often, generational changes in technology impacted the market value for the final product. With Agile, Scrum, and DevOps, technology is evolving generationally every three sprint cycles. Due to the market pace and software release cycles, a modular model for integrating components into a SASE service must be utilized. A modular development and integration model allows the solution to become dynamic by making changes to the security policy or tools so that they can be used consistently within 3 to 5 milliseconds.

Operations Support Systems (OSS) are critical to this implementation in a way that was not previously required. The primary benefit of integrating an OSS with a production solution is the reduction of compounding labor requirements. Essentially, additional scopes are supported with the same labor or less being used.

The modular solution components for integrating IAM into SASE are primarily SASE Services, IAM, MFA, APIs, OSS, Orchestrator, and optionally AIOps. This solution must be implemented with a ZTF

The model we've outlined here allows for systematic, dynamic changes to be made to the architecture on demand. Each solution component may be implemented in either a custom, linear, prescriptive model or in a dynamic, modular model. The former restricts changes and drives both cost and labor components with an average design, build, and deploy time that is greater than 6 weeks. The latter allows a design, build, and deploy time of a single working day. The difference is laying out the architectural model with a permanent API backbone that's connected to each component. This serves as a fixed plumbing system on the A side of the model and the ability to integrate new components on demand on the Z side of the model.

In conclusion, integrating identity systems into SASE should be modular and API-based so that on-demand additions can be made without them impacting the service.

Summary

A multidimensional approach is required to integrate IAM, context, situational components, time of day, location, and many other factors to deliver sub-millisecond, active security that is continuously relevant.

SASE requires IAM to unlock each policy in a ZTF. SASE leverages MFA to act as an enhancement for IAM. Context provides descriptive attributes that may be leveraged to add dimensional layers to security. The situational circumstances around access to a given resource may be grounds for allowing, blocking, or actively shutting down a given SASE session. Situational awareness equips active IPS and AIOps to intervene when necessary. Integrating IAM with SASE must be modular due to the pace of software release cycles. Attaching new products and services in real time must be done on demand and on the same day; it cannot take weeks to implement due to the impact that security threats will have on the organization.

Effective security has always been a layered approach and must now shift to a multi-dimensional solution that scales beyond length, width, and height.

In the next chapter, *Chapter 10, SASE Security*, we will discuss the security that must be inherent in SASE and we will also cover a Secure Overview, Secure Details, Secure Session, Secure Automation, and a Secure Summary.

10
SASE Security

Security can be an elusive concept. To secure a product or service, every part of that product or service must be secure. If any gap in your security exists, it will be exploited, defeating the value that necessitated its purchase. Any organization that gains a poor reputation for security will suffer repercussions that are primarily financial but may extend to legal issues due to follow-on effects. . Effective security provides its own reward in preempting negative consequences to an organization.

SASE provides the opportunity to integrate all security services into a cohesive, interoperating system that is based on a ZTF. In addition to security integration across multiple branded services, SASE is integrated into an organization's entire application, service, and product catalog.

Each software product developer leverages security vertically. In SASE sessions, these vertical solutions must integrate horizontally to form pervasive security, which is necessary for a solution to provide complete security.

In this chapter, we will explain SASE security at a high level, understand the detailed security services in SASE, learn how an SASE session is secured, learn initial options for automating security in SASE, and explain SASE security.

We will cover the following main topics in this chapter:

- Secure Overview – explain SASE security at a high level
- Secure Details – understand the detailed security services in SASE
- Secure Session – learn how the SASE Session is secured
- Secure Automation – learn initial options for automating security in SASE
- Secure Summary – explain SASE security

Secure Overview

The reason that SASE was coined was due to repeated attempts by large organizations to ensure effective security through diverse product portfolios. SASE is the intersection of secure SD-WAN, application security, cloud security, network security, remote access security, data security, and identity security. Secure Access Service Edge provides a framework approach to many different security solutions on the market. Effective security starts with a layered approach, such as a castle, wall, and moat. A ZTF allows a completely blocked resource to become available, as each layer of security is unlocked by meeting each policy requirement for access at that layer.

For the DevOps team, SASE starts with a **Cloud Access Security Broker (CASB)**, **Web Application Firewall (WAF)**, or **Secure Web Gateway (SWG)**. Often, the application development team acquires these solutions outside of procurement processes as part of a cloud platform marketplace offering. Many times, the purchase is tactical and may not work with an organization's overall approach to security, but it allows a project to be completed on time.

For the network infrastructure team, SASE starts with SD-WAN as a replacement for routed solutions which may have a combination of encapsulation that may or may not be secure. Often, the SD-WAN project is treated as a router replacement project that adds little in the way of effective security or network performance. The SD-WAN products on the market often have the key functions needed to be an effective part of a secure communications strategy but bear little resemblance to the previous 30 years of networking solutions. SD-WAN is a key technology to include in a comprehensive SASE Service.

For the security team, SASE starts with next-generation firewall services, and the **Intrusion Prevention System (IPS)** is a key ingredient for both edge and perimeter security. Often, the SWG, CASB, and WAF are managed by DevOps and are outside of a typical security team's operating model. Application-focused security products inconsistently send logs to the **Security Information and Event Management (SIEM)** and a **Security Operations Center (SOC)** for analysis. Seldom are the many SASE Services functions branded, managed, or provided by the same organization. This inconsistency in the operations model prevents effective security.

For the systems team, SASE starts with IAM, which is seldom consistent across devices, applications, services, systems, physical access, and resources. Each organization needs a single source of truth for identity. Integration into legacy systems is challenging but not insurmountable. Once a single identity model is established, it should be considered a universal verification of the who or what, allowing security policy to operate with a ZTF.

SASE is the demarcation point where the differently skilled teams within all organizations need to collapse in one DevSecOps team. This is a call to merge multiple vertical skills into a collective SASE team. For many years, C-level executives have tried to drive business value from their technology teams. Specialization within the technology teams have caused a division of responsibility, effectively working against ideas of ownership. In every organization, security is a required function for every employee to maintain the financial viability of the overall organization. Human safety is almost always considered paramount in the working environment; however, safety does not exist without security. For both the organization's personnel and its financial well-being, effective security is a requirement that must be the responsibility of every employee, contractor, vendor, and partner. If security is everyone's responsibility, then every IT resource has an elevated responsibility to act as part of the security team.

Effective DevSecOps requires effective training. Effective training is not simply a delegation to a third party online or a pre-recorded training. A third-party organization should be used to audit, validate, and certify that individuals and an organization are meeting stated requirements. The responsibility for effective training, however, cannot be delegated. The act of delegation disregards training as a priority and effectively devalues any investment in it.

Effective training requires all levels of an organization to actively participate in focused training that meets the needs of all learning styles. Organizational training must speak to learners who are either visual, auditory, hands-on, or reading and writing-based. Many IT personnel learn best through interactive lab exercises, while other parts of the organization may learn better through pictures, graphs, or charts. Formal academic programs often deliver lecture-based education, which works for some learners. Through writing notes, the value of the lecture may be increased, producing greater retention. Both formal and informal education require significant reading. Each organization has a mixture of learners, and ensuring all learning styles are addressed at each training session may cause frustration and, at the same time, allow each learner to harvest what they need from the session.

Effective leadership in active and visible participation demonstrates value for the outcome of the training. An organization tends to value what its leaders spend their focused time on. Dedicated time by a leader on security training actively reduces organization liabilities. Leadership by example is one of the most cost-effective investments all organizations can make. No amount of financial investment can mitigate the impact of an organization that perceives its leaders as not having time or consideration for security. Perception matters.

In summary, SASE exists for the purpose of secure communications. Today, the market consumes SASE based on role, which increases wastage while reducing security. Effective security requires the integration of all security products or services utilized by an organization with a common IAM. Effective security requires ownership, which requires leadership by example through effective training and visible practices.

In the next section, we will understand the detailed security services in SASE.

Secure Details

Currently, security functions as part of an SASE Service may include any or all the following functions; however, the list at no point in time should be considered exhaustive, as with every product development cycle, more functions will be developed.

The **MEF Forum's SASE Services Definition (MEF W117)** lists the following security functions, with definitions found in the draft standard:

- **Middle Box Function (MBF)**
- **IP, Port, and Protocol Filtering (IPPF)**
- **DNS Protocol Filtering (DPF)**
- **Domain Name Filtering (DNF)**
- **URL Filtering (URLF)**
- **Malware Detection and Removal (MD+R)**
- **Intrusion Prevention System (IPS)**
- **Secure DNS Proxy (SDNSP)**
- **IP Proxy (IP-P)**
- **Data Leakage Prevention (DLP)**
- **Browser Isolation (BI)**

Each function participates in security SASE Services as modular components that can be leveraged by policy for singular and multiple benefits. The number-one priority in SASE is ensuring that a solution is secure. Security can be achieved in a different way by each manufacturer or developer. Each function can be stacked or omitted as needed to cause the desired outcome.

"A middlebox is defined as any intermediary device performing functions other than the normal, standard functions of an IP router on the datagram path between a source host and destination host."

– B. Carpenter. RFC 3234. Middleboxes: Taxonomy and Issues

In summary, the way to achieve prescriptive, secure performance from secure communication solutions is to break services into molecular functions and then trigger each function by policy within an integrated solution.

In the next section, we will learn how an SASE session is secured.

Secure Session

SASE sessions are the core function of an SASE Service. The session is initiated when a user, device, service, or application tries to initiate communications with another user, device, service, or application. The initiator of the session is the subject of the session. The resource being accessed on the remote end is the target. The subject must meet all policy requirements from the ZTF to initiate any communications. The session must be secure to be allowed by policy as an SASE session. Any session that violates the policy must be terminated immediately without waiting for a timeout period.

Each session has a definite starting point and ending point that is managed by an SASE Service. Each session is subject to context, whereby if the context changes, the session must be terminated. Each session is subject to quality requirements, where adverse quality conditions may be considered a potential active threat to security. Each session must be monitored for both security and performance. Each session is defined by a set of SASE specifications that are elements that may be considered and leveraged by policy. Each session must present stateful data to the monitoring system for consideration. Each session is unique and must be treated as such.

All sessions exist as allowed by policy, and if no policy for allowance exists, the session is never established.

Application Flow Specification (**AFS**) was defined by MEF 70.1 to identify the fields and values for classification within a session to be used by policy. The state values within a session allow you to monitor for state changes that may be used by policy to affect an outcome. Session forwarding policies allow traffic to flow through routed or SD-WAN services.

In conclusion, unlike policy-based routing or stateful firewall policies, an SASE session operates based on policy that is dynamic based on the input it receives from attributes, specifications, context, performance, and an increasing set of data to allow for unknown or unanticipated conditions.

In the next section, we will learn about the initial options for automating security in SASE.

Secure Automation

Initial automation of SASE Services can be visualized as AIOps, but the groundwork for the automation must be laid in the form of modular components that may be observed, triggered, operated, and acted upon by the AIOps solution.

A least prescriptive design must be performed, whereby policy is based on loose requirements through small, simple policies. The small simple policies are initially parallel and can be organized hierarchically, from the greatest common denominator to the least common denominator. Each policy should have the ability to stand alone as a module for the AIOps solution to trigger as needed. An **Intrusion Detection System** (**IDS**) detects security threats. An **Intrusion Prevention System** (**IPS**) triggers predetermined reactions to individual threats. AIOps operates on the same principle but cannot be effective with prescriptive reactions to threats. Instead of prescription, a library or catalog of small, singular actions must be created to provide the AIOps system the ability to trigger an action as required, however small it is. The system must be allowed to compound singular actions into sets of serial or parallel actions. After developing the catalog, the system must be tested to allow it to learn naturally, and any undesired effect should be erased and retrained.

The tools of the trade to prepare for automation are orchestration, workflow management, monitoring, telemetry, policy, service management, permissions, testing, training, and an AIOps system.

To summarize, AIOp allows you to automate interaction with a working, secure communications solution to maintain security in real time. Effective automation follows a least-prescriptive design, as the prescriptive approach creates unintended consequences.

In the next section, we will explain SASE security.

Secure Summary

Included in SASE are many security products as well as SD-WAN, which forms the base for the edge extension of the cloud. Depending on the perspective of the team responsible for procuring, designing, implementing, and operating an SASE Service, the initial services may vary. For effective security, all services must be integrated to allow cross-service validation to maintain an even approach to security and mitigating issues that would have increased the threat level.

Key services in a SASE framework include SD-WAN, a firewall, CASB, a ZTF, and SWG. Additional services such as IAM with **Multi-Factor Authentication** (**MFA**) are added out of necessity and must be integrated for effective security. All SASE Services must be integrated to ensure minimum security levels are maintained. All SASE Services must be monitored for both performance and security. Monitoring and telemetry are key inputs for AIOps to interact as needed to ensure policy enforcement.

In conclusion, SASE is security, and without SASE, either significant software development or manual configuration, validation, and intervention are required to ensure security.

Summary

The potential of the future requires diligence in the present to maintain the potential for that future. Without that diligence, the future remains in a state of decline that may disappear at some point. Any science-fiction writer portraying their vision of the future offers hope in the present to change the unintended future into something more intentional. The hope is that our efforts in the present can prevent a future that we do not want.

The viability of any organization in the future is directly connected to its diligence in the present. Security is a key contributor to future success or failure. Each organization must exercise diligence in the present to create the future that they desire. Effective security provides a basis on which to build that future.

In the next chapter, *SASE Services*, examples of many of the services available for SASE integration are discussed, with topics that include: Services Overview, Services Core, Services Options, Services Expanse, and Services Summary.

11
SASE Services

An effective solution is made of many parts that work in concert with each other. A great solution starts to sound more like a symphony. To achieve the desired musical output, the orchestra should have the necessary instruments played by talented masters.

SASE is made up of many different services across multiple technical disciplines or product families. SASE is foundational in its approach to security and may encompass several security services. Secure communications require a service to forward traffic to their destination and, therefore, most solutions require a **Software-Defined Wide Area Network** (**SD-WAN**), but some may be performed across legacy routed environments. An SD-WAN greatly reduces complexity in compliance across the solution, as well as creating a simple policy enforcement integrated services solution.

There are many services that can be included in a **SASE Service**. Every service is not mandatory for a solution to be considered SASE, but every SASE service should have the ability to be integrated into an overall comprehensive solution for a secure connective solution. Potential example services for inclusion are listed here and are expected to evolve as this market matures.

In this chapter, we will get a basic understanding of services in SASE, identify the core services in a SASE solution, catalog optional services that may be incorporated, develop a vision for the expansion of SASE, and learn how to explain SASE services.

We will cover the following main topics in this chapter:

- Services Overview – gain a basic understanding of services in SASE
- Services Core – identify the core services in a SASE solution
- Service Options – catalog optional services that may be incorporated
- Services Expanse – develop a vision for the expansion of SASE
- Services Explain – learn how to explain SASE services

Services Overview

The market will continue to expand in SASE service offerings exponentially for the foreseeable future. Comparable to security software or SD-WAN, the market anticipates growth in the number of services, manufacturers, developers, and service providers of SASE services. During the growth cycle of SD-WAN from 2017 to 2021, close to 100 different SD-WAN products were brought to market. Most products were a single brand or a single product, but several companies brought or acquired several different SD-WAN products, which meant at least 70 companies developed a product.

Today, large resellers have more than 1,000 different security products to sell to their customers as most security practices have brand preferences. Most manufacturers acquire or develop new products as fast as possible to keep up with the feature, function, or tooling requirements of their customers. This activity creates a sprawl in the market offerings and there is an ever-growing expense that creates large gaps between those offerings.

The key differentiator for SASE service offerings from their legacy counterparts is the ability to integrate every service into a cohesive SASE service. This SASE solution must act as one service made of many parts. The effective solution uses the sum of its parts in one whole SASE service. The whole service must use ZTF and must be able to integrate with SD-WAN for a comprehensive solution.

NIST SP 800-207 provides a well-documented understanding of **ZTF** as both **Zero Trust** (**ZT**) and **Zero-Trust Architecture** (**ZTA**). For the purposes of generalization, this book will continue to use ZTF as the focus is to implement a framework approach that will incorporate ZT, ZTA, and **ZTNA**.

Zero Trust Network Access (**ZTNA**) should be thought of as a product or service. ZT is the concept of absolutely no trust within the environment. ZT provides no access to any resource until all required policies for access to each element of the service are satisfied. ZTA should be considered the design approach to integrate products or services into ZTF.

Identifying services that belong in the SASE service-based solution will start with core services that provide foundations on which to integrate all required services. The first SASE service consumed by any organization will be identified based on the needs of that organization and the team within that organization that subscribes to the first SASE service.

Generally, DevOps teams start with CASB, SWG, WAF, or DNS in their approach to SASE. Network teams start with SD-WAN and security teams start with **Firewall-as-a-Service** (**FWaaS**) or ZTNA services. Regardless of the starting point, CIO, CTO, CSO, CISO, CFO, and COO leaders must ensure that the audits of their organization validate the SASE services and their legacy counterparts are fully integrated. The reason that C-level executives must follow up on the SASE consumption within their organization is that failure in this part of the business is not an isolated technology failure but is the largest source of liability in operating any organization. Technical security failure becomes financial and legal failure for the organization. Gross negligence in security may result in imprisonment of the responsible executives.

In summary, SASE services are critical to protecting every organization from liability, business impact, financial impact, loss, and scandal. For this reason, SASE services must be audited for an end-to-end integration to remove gaps in security. Positively, SASE services can and *will* improve security, performance, flexibility in operations, and productivity when implemented correctly. The primary benefit of SASE is the ability to move at the speed of business successfully.

In the next section, we will identify the core services in a SASE solution.

Services Core

From a market perspective, SASE is a secure communications service that solves many of the existing issues with legacy systems. In reality, SASE is a collection of services that each performs an important vertical function, but the value of SASE is when these services are integrated into a single cohesive SASE service.

The core services were initially defined as SD-WAN, CASB, SWG, FWaaS, and ZTNA, as follows:

- SD-WAN is the software-defined secure data forwarding through an encrypted tunnel service.
- CASB is the manager of cloud application security for both access and data loss prevention.
- SWG is the tool that ensures only secure access is used between users and the internet.
- FWaaS is essentially a cloud-based firewall that can be used for both legacy and next-generation firewall capabilities.
- ZTNA is the access tool that provides next-generation capabilities and removes legacy issues from previous remote access tools, such as client access VPN solutions.

The core services are entry points into the SASE service market and are the most common use cases for SASE. For the benefit of security, all SASE services must be identified and integrated into the core services.

All SASE services must participate in the ZTF. In the next section, we will present a catalog of optional services that may be incorporated into a SASE solution.

Service Options

Many services are marketed as "SASE" but may not lend to an integrated ZTF solution. In this section, we will not qualify each solution but discuss SASE services generically, that is, provide examples that may be included in a SASE solution. It's the subscriber of the service that must validate that each service integrates, and ultimately ensure an end-to-end secure communications solution.

SASE Services

The following list is of a catalog of services marketed as SASE services with terms and abbreviations. Many services have been defined or discussed in this book:

- SD-WAN – Software-Defined Wide Area Network
- CASB – Cloud Access Security Broker
- SWG – Secure Web Gateway
- FWaaS – Firewall as a service
- NGFW – Next-Generation Firewall
- ZTNA – Zero-Trust Network Access
- IAM – Identity and Access Management
- MFA – Multifactor Authentication
- DLP – Data Loss Prevention
- EDR – Endpoint Detection and Response
- RBI – Remote Browser Isolation
- SDNS – Domain Name System Filtering/Secure DNS
- MTDR – Managed Threat Detection and Response
- TI – Threat Intelligence
- SIEM – Security Information and Event Management
- AIOPS – Artificial Intelligence for IT Operations (Gartner)
- CSP – Cloud Security Posture
- ADS – Application Delivery Services
- DPS – Device Posture Support
- DM – Device Management
- MDM – Mobile Device Management
- IDPS – Intrusion Detection and Prevention System (IDS/IPS)
- WAN-X – Wide Area Network Acceleration and Optimization
- UBEA – User and Entity Behavior Analytics/User and Event Behavior Analytics
- EP/ES – Endpoint Protection/Endpoint Security
- Anti-X – Anti-Malware/Anti-Virus

Concluding this section, the market has committed to promoting a vast array of services under the term *SASE*. The marketing hype does not lend each product to a SASE service or qualify each service for inclusion in ZTF. The SASE market behavior is similar to legacy data center compute that was branded *cloud compute* with no improvement of services. Each solution must be qualified, tested, integrated, and operated cohesively within the SASE service to provide the benefits of SASE to the organization.

In the next section, we will look at developing a vision for the expansion of SASE.

Services Expanse

SASE shows promise of persistence in the market as terminology technology practitioners will potentially use for secure communications in the same way that "Wi-Fi" has persisted with *IEEE 802.11*. Neither term was a technical contribution to a standard but was once coined as a marketing term and adopted to simplify the discussion of related topics. SASE may be as generic of a term for secure communications as **Internet of Things (IoT)** has become for *device-to-device* communications.

Security Service Edge (SSE) is the latest SASE market variant. SSE is essentially SASE without SD-WAN. Many software and service providers chose to highlight what they consider the next evolutionary step, which is to remove the branch office edge device from the discussion. The primary benefit of SSE as an offer is for sellers that do not have a strong SD-WAN offer. The technical side of the same discussion is that eventually, in a cloud-only approach to IT services, user devices don't need a local private network but instead can use any public internet connection to access all required applications to perform their role in the organization. In this model, the private network of any organization disappears and all access between users, devices, and applications uses ZTF from a cloud-native position.

Cloud application or platform services must be available on the internet for any device or user that requires access. Private networking is now a logical construct through SASE facilitated by application security, which is currently **SSL/TLS**. ZTNA solutions integrated with MFA and MDM pave the way for the next generation in supporting IoT or end user requirements for access.

Blockchain, distributed ledger, or Web 3.0 solutions will depend upon SASE services to harvest validated identity as well as context verification. Each ledger entry will need to collect and verify information that will become a permanent part of the transactions in every case.

As an example, digital logistics transactions may require a waypoint signature from a package in transit which is validated with the right information\answer of the questions. Who is transporting the package? What is being transported? Is it the original package? Is the original item in the package? Has the package been opened? What is the temperature of the package? Where is the package? The answer to the *where* question is to create logs for each mile marker on the way as a waypoint. What time was the package at the waypoint? Based on the current progress, what is the predicted arrival time to the minute? What other types of packages were in proximity to the relevant package? Are there additional data points required for customer needs? Each answer becomes a permanent record on the ledger. The SASE service provides validated attributes that will become a reliable part of the ledger system to ensure devices, users, and applications become solid forensic contributions to the blockchain.

IoT solutions will continue to mature across many generations for both hardware and software. Many different marketing terms will try to describe variants of IoT solutions creating a market sprawl. As the IoT market evolves, it becomes more dependent upon secure communications solutions such as SASE. Many SASE services, such as device management solutions, will depend on SASE as a way of validating machine identity, authenticating the machine through MFA, verifying context, allowing communications across specific protocols to specific applications, and allowing only specific operations personnel access to change their policies. Much of the future depends on generic base configurations that are dependent upon ZTF to unlock access one layer at a time. In the past, prescription of configuration was considered effective security but has consistently proven ineffective. Security still requires a layered approach, but the future is not only layered in approach but is multi-dimensional as well.

To summarize, the future will provide SASE services with thousands of variants of service options that may be included within the SASE concept. Each organization must see through the hype to validate solutions that fully integrate with a cloud-native ZTF. In the next section, we will learn how to explain SASE services to those unfamiliar with SASE.

Services Explain

SASE is a secure communications framework for integrating security solutions that are based on a **Zero-Trust Framework (ZTF)** to achieve effective secure communications.

When explaining SASE at the executive level, explain it as a cloud based, secure communications service that replaces many of your firewall, WAN, remote access, and application security products. When explaining it to security, network, or application development teams, **SASE**, or **Secure Access Service Edge**, is the next-generation way of combining cloud security, firewall security, and network security. It allows for interdependent security policies to become effective.

SASE-based services provide integrated security policies for all IT-based solutions. Each service in its legacy form was a stand-alone service that may have been sold as the only service purchased by the subscriber at that time. The challenge has been to develop a comprehensive security offering that allows for effective secure communications. The effective discussion has been a multiple-decade moving target. Many technology vendors have benefited from the confusion and sprawl resulting from offering supplemental services for network, application, and security solutions. While financially beneficial from an initial transaction perspective, the long-term costs in both liability and maintenance have pushed the market to seek an integrated approach such as SASE.

Summary

SASE service should be considered a marketing term that depends on security engineering teams to validate compliance with a fully integrated ZTF.

The requirement for effective security drives the requirement for a fully integrated solution that combines every attribute we can collect and identify. Each attribute can then be included in policy-based decisions to allow secure communications. The more we can learn about the answers to *who*, *what*, *when*, *why*, and *where*, the more effective the policies become.

There is no future model that allows discrete, disparate, divided, disjoined, or disintegrated technology-based services. Each service must be interdependent for an effective policy.

In the next chapter, we will look into establishing, monitoring, and enforcing the configuration, policy, and performance of any given component of SASE, or the SASE overall solution.

12
SASE Management

In the past, many systems were deployed without effective management. This oversight, while obvious today, was not always intentional or thoughtless in nature. Effective management systems have not always been available. Early management tools were costly while only managing minor portions of a system in production. Management systems were commonly seen as a luxury, due to costs with limited value and poor understanding.

Today, it is not possible to provide effective and secure communications without management, as a static configuration does not guarantee security, nor does it guarantee performance. Dynamic management systems, tools, processes, and automation are required for persistent security and performance. Without automation, labor costs multiply as compared to previous generations of technology. Without proper tooling, compliance becomes an ongoing project cost. Without templates, the quantity of required labor increases, and qualified labor sources are rare in the market since the technology is still new. This increases labor rates.

By taking the time and budget to implement **SASE Management** properly, the labor required to maintain, audit, and renew SASE services will decrease annually. Each effectively used management tool will improve effectiveness with each iteration.

In *Chapter 3*, *SASE Managed*, we focused on the management model. In this chapter, we will discuss the topics of *establishing*, *monitoring*, and *enforcing* the configuration, policy, and performance of any given component of the SASE overall solution.

We will cover the following main topics in this chapter:

- Management Overview – learn the approach to managing SASE
- Management Systems – explain the management options and their functions
- Management Templates – take the template approach to scaling
- Management Automation – automate management functions
- Management Simplified – explain SASE Management

Management Overview

The approach to managing SASE should be novel when compared to previous systems. For many years, IT professionals have striven to create effective management systems, ultimately finding the solution elusive. Today, taking lessons learned from the telecommunications service providers, we leverage the concept of **service orchestration** beyond manufacturer-specific tools. Service orchestration is not new but is commonly misrepresented in marketing language to drive revenue.

For the purposes of SASE management, each manufacturer provides one or more orchestrators, element managers, management tools, or other systems for the purpose of managing one or more SASE services. The challenge presented here is that many organizations may have several dozen SASE services in production requiring separate orchestration. The complexity of service management and the need to implement solutions in real time are the two primary reasons for outsourcing SASE management.

Effective SASE management requires a master orchestration platform, API management, service management, **Artificial Intelligence for IT Operations** (**AIOps**), service level management, and cost management tools. Over time, more components may be required, but it is important that a large structure is planned to easily integrate new services in an on-demand fashion. The on-demand approach should be designed in a way where any required service may be fully implemented, within any size of organization within a single day.

While a single-day timeline will immediately be challenged by every person involved, the liability of a security threat is the first reason that this timeline is the most cost-effective for every organization. Speed of execution can protect an organization from security threats. On-demand upgrades are necessary for security integrity.

The second reason for the timeline is that if it takes longer than a day to implement the design for the SASE Service, it is ineffective. The ineffective nature of a solution that takes weeks or months to implement is that software development lifecycles produce required code potentially every sprint cycle. While no organization implements new code every few weeks or every release, an organization that takes months to implement code will be perpetually several generations behind the standard on security, performance, and enhancement features. The overall design of a SASE service must be a design that allows same-day installations for any one service.

Identifying an ineffective solution is easy. Verbalizing or documenting ineffective solution components is more challenging. Most organizations have to move on quickly to the next project, which leaves the ineffective nature of the last project as a crack in the foundation that becomes harder to fix over time.

Legacy network, security, and application systems require months to implement correctly, whereas, at the time of writing, an average software-defined solution can be implemented in less than one hour. Organizational processes, institutional education, and personnel development have not evolved at the pace of the market. On the market, the average *Kubernetes Pod* may only exist for 2 minutes. That Pod may have been a router, a firewall, a wireless controller, a database, an application, or some other necessary system that was designed, built, deployed, used, and recycled in less time than it takes to cook popcorn in a microwave oven.

Each of these concepts is presented to illustrate how human management of effective secure communications is an impossible task. The policy leveraged by the machine that must perform all these requirements for secure communications is the critical human contributed component. There must be an emotional separation from the desire for perfection in SASE. That human desire to provide the *best* is necessary and valued highly but must be refocused on iteration.

Simple iterative development is that which produces a minimum viable product that is 85–90% of conceivable perfection and provides useful value. The very next iteration must be around 87–92% of perfection. Iteration three becomes 89–94% of perfection. Every addition iteration must strive to be a 1–2% improvement over the previous iteration, as perfection is ultimately unachievable, and the market brands that achieve the highest levels of perfection on the market have ceased to exist through bankruptcy or other forms of failure. In many cases, products have outlived their creator organizations by 20 and, in some cases, more than 100 years.

The pursuit of perfection is extremely valuable, but the market seldom pays for the cost of that perfection. A solution that is good enough for use will provide a modest profit, whereas solutions on the brink of perfection bankrupt companies. Often, the market will pay better for better solutions, but the point of no financial return is hard to predict.

In *Chapter 3, SASE Managed*, the following management tools were documented as a minimum foundation for SASE management:

- **Master Orchestration Platform**: This will be the **Multi-Domain Service Orchestrator** (**MSDO**) that maintains a push/pull relationship with individual services or product orchestrators.

- **Network Management System**: The **Network Management System** (**NMS**) is typically what an SD-WAN vendor calls its orchestrator.

- **API Manager**: Almost every software-based product today has an **Application Programming Interface** (**API**) library available for rapid integration. To effectively scale automation and integrations, a management platform is needed to function as a spine to maintain structure for the individual API of each function integrated.

- **Service Management Platform**: Integrating via an API and collecting logging at all levels, collecting quality measurement data, collecting reporting information, collecting SLA measurement data, and integrating architectural design knowledge and any other feedback into a central location is key to all operational decisions.

- **Artificial Intelligence Operations Platform (AIOps)**: **AIOps** will combine all available data as well as machine training models to dynamically learn from gaps or failures.

- **Service Level Management**: The tool for managing a **Service-Level Agreement** (**SLA**) is necessary, as it provides the standard by which effective service operations are measured.

- **Cloud Cost Management**: Deploying an effective cost management solution allows for real-time cost feedback that can comply with the SLA.

SASE management is both more complicated and valuable to an organization than previous management systems. If correctly designed and implemented, SASE management can reduce costs for an organization significantly but requires a change in the fundamental IT processes of that organization. In the next section, we will learn about the management options and their functions.

Management Systems

Orchestration is a requirement for SASE, as human intervention to security threats or active attacks is not possible. It is not possible for the IT staff of an organization to both detect an attack and stop it within 2 milliseconds. The actual goal should be for attacks to be stopped within one tenth of a millisecond. Effective SASE design can achieve this goal.

The **master orchestration** platform should be something that will consolidate and collect telemetry from downstream orchestration, while interacting in a push/pull relationship with subordinate orchestration platforms. The *master orchestrator* must be able to share all collected knowledge with the SIEM as well as all other integrated service components with their respective tools.

API management should go beyond catalog services and provide policy compliance with permanent API backbone services. The API backbone should be a permanent construction that provides constant access to all available APIs for any SASE service or tool system. Instead of deploying an API per requirement or per use case, all available APIs are published to a common backbone so that the next deployed service takes advantage of the existing implementations instead of developing a new solution every time a service is added.

In the case of many service management platforms, incident management and change management are the only two modules deployed. Problem management is often overseen outside of the platform. With SASE services, the other modules provide data necessary for input into the policy, automation, performance, and AIOps components of the service.

AIOps should be something well beyond the idea of ticket or event correlation. AIOps must be an active read/write part of an overall SASE framework. The AIOps solution components must include a dedicated platform outside of the other services but should fully integrate with the AIOps components built into or provided with each SASE service in an overall SASE solution. The existence of AIOps as a dedicated platform outside each AIOps service component allows for a third-wheel mechanism to act as tie breakers for conflicts as the authoritative AI decision-maker in the solution. To be clear, AIOps in this context means autonomous incident, event, problem, change, and intervention resolution without human assistance.

The **Artificial Intelligence** (**AI**) system resolves any task that would have required a human to perform. AI has the ability to and must be authorized to perform pre-approved actions in response to any type of ticket logged or event detected. Today, many intrusion prevention platforms sit idle due to the fear of false positive situations that would shut down communications until manual intervention. Autonomous systems have been used successfully for more than 10 years at the time of writing. Success will require planning and, ultimately, the release of control to a system to execute pre-approved actions.

The simplest way to prepare is to have the change control board oversee a sandboxed lab testing of each automation. As each automation is shown to have no adverse or unintended consequences, a change control board is convened to approve each automation in production.

Service level management is necessary for contractual obligations but is also a reliable source of performance metrics for SASE services to correct performance issues. Many SASE service developers provide an API to interconnect systems that provide external SLA visibility. A fully managed service should provide reporting on SLA attainment metrics, and a well-managed service will leverage these metrics to increase performance as it relates to **User Experience** (**UX**).

Cloud computing created a revival in cost management tools for many types of services. SASE management must include cost management for tools, increasing variable costs such as *hybrid* and *public* cloud-based tools.

To conclude this section, the management platforms must perform a complex, compound, and interlocking service mesh that leaves nothing unaccounted for. In the past, management tools only contributed to costs as ancillary utilities. Future SASE management platforms can provide innovative cost reduction over the life of any SASE service while increasing performance of the overall solution.

In the next section, we will take a templated approach to scaling.

Management Templates

Microsoft Office applications *Word*, *Excel*, and *PowerPoint* offer value primarily because their formats are considered universal for exchanging information between and within organizations around the world. Within any organization, iteration based on common templates reduces rework, often above the 99% level in the case of repetitive processes.

The top 10 consulting companies in the world have built massive profitability into performing research once and leveraging it countless times through a templated and extremely well-educated process.

Automobile manufacturers, thanks in great part to Henry Ford, have maximized shareholder value by creating a template for each part of each specific model of automobile they intend to manufacture. Leveraging the template, the manufacturer assembles the parts into a compound and complex final product that reduces the cost of manufacturing each automobile by a factor of ten or more.

The technology industry has mastered the art of the template. We take solution components that were built using a templated process. Unfortunately, many organizations consciously try to implement them in a custom manner. This custom implementation reduces the benefit of the templates used to produce products that are configured uniquely.

SD-WAN and SASE are complex technologies that leverage policies that may be templated to accelerate the design, building, deployment, and operation of those services. Leveraging a template with a least-prescriptive design allows for multiple templates to be compounded for an orchestrator to achieve the desired outcome. An SLA cannot be achieved through prescription because the world is not static but severely dynamic. No network, application, or security solution provides value in a lab. The value is provided in production where all conditions vary based on external environmental and performance variations. Not even the electricity used to bring the SASE service to life is predictable or fixed in any behavior. Policies for any given service may prescribe behavior, but the best way to achieve the desired outcome is through a hierarchical model built upon multiple, simple, least-prescriptive policies.

SASE Templates

Each SASE service can be designed, built, deployed, and operated with a *template-driven* approach. Each template should be painfully simple with as little policy as possible.

Like the process of teaching a child to bake a cake for the first time, each policy template must take our cake recipe and divide it into many smaller tasks. A cake recipe with 5 steps becomes a 1,000-step process; not for the sake of overproduction but for the sake of teaching the AI. The simplification of steps into smaller components is a necessary part of the solution of how to bake a cake for the first time, every time.

This idea of using many hundreds of smaller steps to achieve something that we might achieve in 30 lines of configuration may seem massively overwhelming and misguided. Like the carpenter that measures twice and cuts once, we avoid waste. An effective template-based design for the first 10 sites in an SD-WAN deployment can implement the next 10,000 sites in the same elapsed time as the first 10 sites.

Consider that the average consumer network device is installed in increments of hundreds of thousands of devices in one day through simple design and a great UX. Conversely, complex design is not the friend of a cost-conscious organization while delivering a poor UX.

Concluding this section, creating templates that take complex solutions and break them into many smaller pieces enables automation at a scale that has rarely been seen. In the next section, we will learn how to automate management functions.

Management Automation

The *automation* of management functions is simple in that it requires permission granted in advance to perform up to 95% of all management functions and the autonomy to do so.

Most management platforms today offer libraries full of automation that are never used due to fear. While identified as risk or liability management, the enactment of a fear-driven process negates the sunk cost of the automated features of almost every piece of software.

Plan for automation! In the process of developing change control governance, each organization must create boundaries around what automations are acceptable to the organization. If the answer is none, the organization is missing cost reductions that have already been paid for and that may be realized through simple planning and testing.

To prepare for automation approvals, each automation must be tested in a non-production environment with manufacturer support, with lessons learned being documented. The honesty of the documented results should provide an opportunity for all reasonable change control boards to approve automated changes in a production environment. Each successful month of automations causing no impact on an organization should allow additional automations to gain approval. If some automations continue to cause issues, a temporary suspension of those types of automations is required, and a root-cause analysis should be performed. Well-performing automations should not be punished due to poor performers. Technical staff should constantly test and innovate with new automations, as each new level of automation has the potential to improve UX, reduce costs, and free up labor to create business value.

To conclude, an automation must be an innovative part of every SASE service as talented resources must be able to scale to new evolving organizational requirements. Without automation, adequate labor may never exist to solve the growing number of challenges that continue to outpace available labor sources.

In the next section, we will learn about SASE management.

Management Simplified

When explaining SASE management, it is common to state similarities to network, security, and application management. In many cases, a simple high-level definition should be both common-sense and provide a quick overview. The simple definition also has the consequence of impacting funding by underestimating compound licensing requirements or extensive labor needs to establish effective management. SASE management requires more labor to establish effective management, but through automation and AIOps, the costs of compliance labor, operations labor, and life cycle refresh labor can be reduced.

SASE management, the simple model; element or service management plus orchestration with templating and automation tools.

Summary

SASE management is more complex to build than the management of previous services, as policies must interlock to provide effective secure communication. A systematic, hierarchical, template-based, and automated approach to SASE management can pave the way for unprecedented levels of scale to manage the evolving needs of any organization. Putting more effort into the initial design and deployment of a management platform and its supporting systems can reduce costs, labor, and compliance efforts.

If the concept of baking a cake with 1,000 mini-tasks to complete causes you concern, it should. There is no feasible way for a human to complete the increasing level of tasks required for managing any environment in real-time. A combination of DevOps practices with effective management systems (that include orchestration and AIOps) is required to achieve success. The automated systems break working environments if complex or compound policies are utilized. Each process has to be broken into a mini-task (or even a nano-task) such as an individual musical note on a single instrument in the world's largest orchestra playing a symphony. The orchestrator assembles the players, instruments, talent, music, and then empowers each musician to play the correct note at the correct time, which results in beauty for all who hear it.

In the next chapter, we will give you an overview of SASE Stakeholders and discuss them from from an Overview, Business, Technical, User, and Success perspectives.

Part 3 – SASE Success Perspective

Part 3 leverages lessons learned from successful SASE projects. This section provides insights from a technical program management perspective to ensure a successful SASE implementation.

In this section, there are the following chapters:

- *Chapter 13, SASE Stakeholders*
- *Chapter 14, SASE Case*
- *Chapter 15, SASE Design*
- *Chapter 16, SASE Trust*

13
SASE Stakeholders

Every great project starts from a primary goal or objective that is achieved through expert planning, discipline, execution, and validation post-completion. In this way, SASE Service projects are similar as all stated elements are required. SASE differs from most projects in the level of collaboration and overall input required from key **stakeholders**.

Stakeholders are simply those that have something to either lose or gain from the project's outcome.

In every successful project, the key stakeholders must be defined so that their definition of success is recorded before planning the work effort. Success criteria must be written and agreed to in the beginning and the overall project must be measured by its achievement of those written criteria.

Project failure can be financial or physical in nature, related to UX, dangerous, or just perceived by the key stakeholders. Perception is the hardest to fight but must be fought for the sake of the organization the project is to benefit. Clearly stated in writing, goals, objectives, and success criteria must be the actual measurement and without both, pre-statement and post-analysis success is stillborn.

In this chapter, we will discuss why stakeholders are so important to SASE, who should be involved from the business team, who should be involved from the technical team, and what role the SASE users play in decisions, and explain stakeholder success for SASE.

In this chapter, we will cover the following main topics:

- Stakeholders Overview – why are stakeholders so important to SASE
- Stakeholders Business – who should be involved from the business team
- Stakeholders Technical – who should be involved from the technical team
- Stakeholder Users – what role do the SASE users play in decision making
- Stakeholder Success – explain stakeholder success for SASE

Stakeholders Overview

Why are stakeholders so important to SASE? The simple answer is that SASE policies are used for secure communications to devices, applications, and resources for each user within an organization starting with ZTF. No access from any user or device to any application, system, or network of any kind is the default. For access, a policy must be created that allows it. Effective security comes at the price of conscious effort.

ZTF is not like traditional configuration or blacklist firewall functionality. **Zero Trust** equals **Zero Access** until the policy allows access. This is not an intuitive thought process. ZTF is the right solution but is like having individual locks on everything in the pantry. Your fingerprint might open everything except someone else's special treat that only works with their fingerprint.

Zero is the starting point in the journey and each organization can define its journey but requires input from key stakeholders as to what should be permitted. Without expressed permission in a policy, the default answer is *no*.

SASE Stakeholders must be defined at the beginning of the project and any part of the organization not represented will not have access to the resources accessed by the SASE Service. Start with the question of *who* or *what* needs access to the service, identifying the decision maker for each resource accessed. This may be one or hundreds of stakeholders, depending on the service being implemented.

Common stakeholders represent the network, security, application, and business interests in the SASE Service being implemented. Stakeholders should also include UX test representatives as any service with poor UX will not last long enough to provide a **Return on Investment** (**ROI**).

To sum things up, SASE stakeholders include representation from any part of the organization that requires access or is impacted through the SASE Service. In the next section, we will discuss who should be involved from the business team.

Stakeholders Business

Often, business stakeholders are represented by technology resources, but in the case of SASE Services, it is critical to involve the business stakeholders within the organization to define expectations from a UX perspective, as well as the business value requirements. With legacy systems being replaced by SASE, open access to systems was a default expectation that ultimately caused security vulnerabilities. With ZTF, the SASE Service will restrict all access to the new service or its resources until a policy exists that provides access. For this reason, the business needs to define expectations in a concise but comprehensive document. Success and test criteria should be defined at the point of receipt of the business expectations document.

Business value is the key expectation of technology departments. When that expectation is met, the organization invests in technology-based solutions. The opposite is also true as each organization has finite resources that must be allocated based on value. Many CIO compensation plans focus on metrics or **Key Performance Indicators** (**KPIs**) that are tied to UX. Pay to perform is becoming a more common practice to relate how business value is impacted by the end UX from any service within an organization.

Business stakeholders should be involved early and often to achieve a positive and productive UX. Many of the current issues being addressed by SASE Service integration through orchestration are due to the current **Software-as-a-Service** (**SaaS**) sprawl where business stakeholders who, through frustration or impatience with legacy IT practice, went around the IT department and purchased SaaS solutions directly. Unfortunately, this bypassed effective security practices and SLA measurement. In discussing this issue with many organizations, the struggle is primarily to identify, inventory, and account for every service or application their organization is consuming. This practice creates an impossible challenge for compliance. Forcing an organization to forgo productivity and care for external customers is ineffective as it competes directly with the existential purpose of the organization. Instead of force, strong customer service practices by the IT department's leadership team can motivate key stakeholders to choose to integrate external services with a strong-performing SASE Service. By serving internal customers successfully, the productivity, performance, quality, and compliance of the organization are benefited.

All in all, you would need to engage the business stakeholders positively through beneficial education and strong customer service practices. In the next section, we will discuss who should be involved from the technical team.

Stakeholders Technical

The **technical stakeholders** should be apparent but may be elusive in this context. Security, network, systems, applications, DevOps, administrators, program management, helpdesk, and management are all easy to identify but often not included in project planning.

SASE policies are based on ZTF, and no access exists until a policy is developed and implemented that allows access to the resource defined in the policy. For this reason, *every part* of the organization must be considered for policy development input.

Examples of Technical **SASE Service** dependencies that may not have been required by previous technology-based solutions are as follows:

- Compliance teams will need a data feed from the policy enforcement points
- Accounting will need to ensure variable costs flow to the responsible departmental budget
- Legal departments need to ensure no undocumented extension of liability exists
- Human resource teams must be precise to the minute on personnel starts, stops, or role changes

- Physical security has physical access integration requirements tied to IAM and facility access systems
- Business operations need accurate timing for digital signatures that may be added to distributed ledgers as part of contracted performance metrics such as customer SLA/SLO
- Logistics must keep accurate timestamps for when and where anything is moving or being stored for the organization, as well as who accesses what

Previously, each of these examples would have been considered business stakeholders and must still be considered so. In addition to the business requirements, the systems supporting the business stakeholders have expanded technical requirements that drive the additional need for technical decision-making inclusion by business stakeholder administrative teams.

Operational Technology (OT) is a term that mainly focuses on manufacturing technology – typically, machine control systems. The line between IT and OT has blurred beyond recognition. The line continues to blur with distributed ledger technology that requires input from both physical and logical systems to carry out business transactions both internal and external to each organization.

Concluding this section, technical stakeholder identification continues to evolve as the entire organization becomes a technical organization, regardless of the technical nature of the organization's purpose. Next, we are going to discuss what role SASE users play in decisions.

Stakeholder Users

The value of any solution without a positive user experience should be considered zero. The profitability leader in almost any category is the one with the most positive UX. A profitable organization with poor UX has asymmetric value controls over its revenue source. Examples of both types of entities are available through personal experience and are in great supply.

A positive and productive focus should be on the positive UX category for the primary justification of ROI. Within non-profit and governmental organizations, the ROI for positive user interaction with the organization is manifested in funding increases that may not be forecasted. Natural laws observed provide positive ROI for altruistic investments. For profit-seeking organizations, the financial benefits are more quickly realized for positive UX.

Positive UX provides intangible benefits to every organization through more subtle sources such as reduced incidents, escalations, and administrative burdens. Leadership compensation has a strong trend toward UX-related KPIs, which allows all levels of the organization to prioritize UX when implementing or operating new solutions.

When developing a new project, the UX must be represented by both leadership and end user communities to develop both success and test criteria. Project and program management teams must create a dedicated workstream that allows the end user experience to be treated as a primary form of project success.

UX is a key, if not the key measurement, by which any SASE Service should be measured for success, so the end user community needs to be represented in project planning as well as in post-project validation exercises. In the next section, we will learn how to explain stakeholder success for SASE.

Stakeholder Success

While developing a project, the *project charter* must include key stakeholder input for success criteria. Success criteria must be documented before committing labor to a project as the skills and quantities of labor required are greatly affected by how success is measured. Testing the success criteria must occur before, frequently during, and after the project is completed to evaluate its success.

Success is still a subjective term, but the financial success of each project is based on finite criteria and must be measured by its achievement. The UX after project completion drives the perceived project success and ultimately affects the funding of the next project.

Summary

Success for SASE stakeholders is tied to policy development and enforcement. To develop SASE policies, all key stakeholders must be consulted for their input regarding what they consider project success to be. Policy development must consider UX as the perception of success will be defined in UX.

In the next chapter, we will review the Overview, Insight, Examples, Design, and Value of the *use* or *business cases* for SASE.

14
SASE Case

With every new generation of technology, a new method of understanding is needed to employ the innovative technology effectively and beneficially. Education is based on historical context with a limited understanding of what the future may look like. The Use Case method may be the best way to understand how to design solutions in the SASE generation of services..

When we study history, we can see predictive patterns appear that provide insight into the future, but the actual details about the future are unclear. Scientific analysis of the present shows that the present was ultimately predictable. Failure to understand history creates both present and future failure. How, if this is so complicated, can we be successful in designing a secure communications service with SASE?

The answer to SASE design success is in understanding the SASE Use Case.

In this chapter, we will discuss what a Use Case is, how Use Cases affect SASE, some examples of SASE Use Case, how to design Use Cases, and the Use Cases value propositions for SASE.

In this chapter, we will cover the following main topics:

- Case Overview – what is an use Case
- Case Insight – how does the Use Case affect SASE
- Case Examples – what are examples of SASE Use Cases
- Case Design – how to design Use Cases
- Case Value – explain Use Case value propositions for SASE

Case Overview

What is a Use Case? A Use Case is a method of explaining how the final solution will be used. By describing its use, the policy and design can be developed in a relevant and meaningful way.

When researching the term **Use Case**, the definitions varied extensively. Multiple definitions that fit the context of this discussion revolved around the scientific or medical definitions of the term. Essentially, Use Case is a term used differently by each profession. In medical definitions, there is a study-based approach to understanding the context for the use and the result of that use. This approach allows the same product or solution to be used in separate ways to accomplish specific outcomes.

The market does not have a common definition of a SASE Use Case. Each SASE Service interprets the words *Use Case* in a different context. This ambiguity of these words is not problematic – it is simply a matter of perspective. This book does not define a Use Case authoritatively; instead, it uses the concept to present a design methodology that enables the rapid design of SASE-based solutions.

Developing multiple Use Cases allows for a simpler understanding of the success criteria from the perspective of each Use Case requirement. Once each Use Case has been solutioned, the macro-level design supports all the requirements. Complex design requirements often stall progress within SASE projects as every possible user requirement combined creates an impossible-to-design-for problem. By breaking the requirements down into smaller pieces by visualizing a singular Use Case, the problem becomes simpler to solve and, ultimately, manageable by the project team.

In the past, the final policy that was implemented had to be comprehensive in the final production configuration. Today, the policy becomes comprehensive in production through solving each Use Case individually and allowing orchestration to execute the solution for each Use Case, as well as allowing interactive security solutions to intervene on demand.

Prescriptive policy design, which is a type of design that accounts for and controls every eventuality, is ignorant of the past, present, and future. *It is not possible to design for every possible situation. It is not possible to design for every possible situation. It is not possible to design for every possible situation.* This has been repeated multiple times to reiterate a point that you already know but may not have verbalized within your organization. We cannot design a policy that solves every threat, problem, risk, scenario, performance goal, or eventuality. Thankfully, it is not necessary to design for every possible situation.

We design for all intended Use Cases, orchestrate, automate, and insert AIOps in both the performance and security policy. After we design correctly, we *allow* the solution to dynamically solve problems that we did not envision. This often requires preplanning change control to allow for potential service-affecting interactions with the AIOps solution. The preplanning is worth the struggle to adapt the organization's culture to end security or performance issues at the point of origin in real time. An effective SASE solution will act upon the policy within the session or at the first malicious packet. Human intervention takes minutes, hours, days, or weeks, depending on the organization's policy, tools, skills, and available resources.

In summary, a Use Case is a tool or method that allows us to focus on the **Minimum Viable Product (MVP)** that can be built upon as needed to carry out the solution envisioned in the Use Case.

In the next section, we will discuss how the use case method affects SASE.

Case Insight

Effective SASE design focuses on user requirements, as well as building upon ZTF. The Use Case should supply a visualization of the desired outcome from an end user perspective. The UX should be considered the ultimate quality and performance indicator for the solution. Security from ZTF is inherent and therefore the design goal is to not inhibit ZTF.

Effective compensation for SASE teams should be tied to UX. SASE is a common way of supplying secure communications for end users, devices, and systems to enable organizations to serve their customers. Without a positive user experience, customers, and ultimately your financial success is impacted. Positive UX can only be provided through effective security and for this reason, both concepts are symbiotic and indivisible.

How does a Use Case affect SASE? A Use Casee ultimately makes SASE a concept that can be digested in bite-sized pieces. Designing an MVP for a specific use case allows the architect to develop a SASE working MVP service. Success is based on the iteration as opposed to engineering perfection. Start from ZTF and unlock resources via the policy until the MVP is achieved on the first Use Case to achieve MVP on the SASE Service. More Use Cases may be bolted on without fear of missing something as the orchestration can compound policy components to achieve specific policy enforcement. Through implementing each Use Case to the policy via MVP approaches, multiple levels of compounding policy can be achieved to support multiple Use Cases.

The policy mustn't be developed in a finite or compound way as this prohibits the value of orchestration, AIOps, and future generations of security intervention.

In summary, the Use Case method makes SASE simpler to design, build, implement, and operate.

In the next section, we will discuss examples of SASE Use cases.

Case Examples

In this section, we will outline Use Cases examples for a common frame of reference when developing specific Use Cases. There are no exhaustive lists of Use Cases as no such thing is possible. SASE will continue to evolve for decades, including more services.

Each Use Case definition is simplistic by design and should only be used as an ideation or starting point for you to develop a Use Case template.

SD-WAN – Software-Defined Wide Area Network:

- **What**: Secure *site-to-site, site-to-cloud, or site-to-internet* communications that replace routing or a router with a physical appliance, VNF, or CNF running software-defined networks.
- **Who**: Systems, offices, home offices, data centers, partner sites, **Cloud Service Providers** (**CSP**), or other physical and virtual locations that are needed to take part in a private network.
- **Where**: Anywhere in the world.

- **How**: Endpoint-to-endpoint encryption using TLS or IPSEC tunneling with dynamic tunneling over both the internet and MPLS connections via any carrier and any circuit type. All applications in scope offer acceptable performance at 120 ms or less.
- **When**: All endpoints are allowed access at any time of day, but idle users are to be disconnected after each session is terminated with system MFA-based reauthentication on a per-session basis while leveraging ZTF.
- **Why**: This solution needs to provide secure communications access to applications to support the organization's internal and external customers.

FWaaS – Firewall as a Service:

- **What**: A firewall that's hosted externally to the organization and paid for as a service by a third party. This security system may be a cloud-based firewall that is replicated or distributed globally with policy synchronization.
- **Who**: Employees, contractors, partners, systems, devices, or services that need access to resources to perform their organizational function will be supplied with secure communications to the organization's network, systems, or applications.
- **Where**: Access or endpoints may be located anywhere in the world.
- **How**: FWaaS will enforce logical boundaries where they are defined through any available internet connection. End users must use MFA through ZTF to access the applications. The highest allowed encryption per country is required. When one country's requirements are lower than the corporate standard, access from that country will be through an additional remediation DMZ. All applications in scope offer acceptable performance at 120 ms or less.
- **When**: All users are allowed access at any time of day, but idle users are to be disconnected after each session is terminated with system MFA-based reauthentication on a per-session basis while leveraging ZTF.
- **Why**: This solution is required to defend organizational information systems boundaries, as defined by the policy. It must be synchronized across all FWaaS instances.

ZTNA – Zero Trust Network Access:

- **What**: A remote access VPN replacement built to allow ZTF-based access to both cloud and on-premises applications.
- **Who**: Employees, contractors, and partners who need access to specific applications to perform their organizational functions will be provided secure communications to the organization's applications.
- **Where**: End users may be located anywhere in the world.

- **How**: End users will use mobile devices such as smartphones, tablets, and laptops to access applications through any available internet connection. End users must use MFA through ZTF to access the applications. The highest allowed encryption per country is required, where one country's requirements are lower than the corporate standard; access from that country will be through an additional remediation DMZ. All applications in scope offer acceptable performance at 120 ms or less.
- **When**: All users are allowed access at any time of day, but idle users are to be disconnected after each session is terminated with system MFA-based reauthentication on a per-session basis while leveraging ZTF.
- **Why**: This solution must provide secure communications access to applications to support the organization's internal and external customers.

In conclusion, each of these Use Cases is a high-level example. Depending on the organization, the use case method may evolve as the requirements or technology evolve. The important rule to remember is to assign each use case to an MVP and the policy they produce to an MVP. The more elaborate or prescriptive each policy is, the less the organization benefits from automation and AIOps.

In the next section, we'll discuss how to design use cases.

Case Design

To design the Use Case, first, start with the end state production goals in mind. The Use Case must be defined concerning the UX. Identify the who, what, where, how, when, and why of the use case's requirements.

In the following Use Case, think about what could be refined or added to better describe the experience goal. The end user gets sub-120 ms access to any application, anywhere, at any time, from three different device types. The security limits from ZTF are expanded to allow sub-optimal encryption and that traffic is remediated through a DMZ. Security also allows MFA, which is both a convenience and a risk mitigator through a policy. The why is defined as a high-level justification for the service to be provided as each service carries a risk that must be accounted for and mitigated.

Example Use Case

ZTNA – Zero Trust Network Access:

- **What**: A remote access VPN replacement built to allow ZTF-based access to both cloud and on-premises applications.
- **Who**: Employees, contractors, and partners who need access to specific applications to perform their organizational function will be provided secure communications to the organization's applications wherever they may be located.
- **Where**: End users may be located anywhere in the world.

- **How**: End users will use mobile devices such as smartphones, tablets, and laptops to access applications through any available internet connection. End users must use MFA through ZTF to access the applications. The highest allowed encryption per country is required, where one country's requirements are lower than the corporate standard; access from that country will be through an additional remediation DMZ. All applications in scope offer acceptable performance at 120 ms or less.

- **When**: All users are allowed access at any time of day, but idle users are to be disconnected after each session is terminated with system MFA-based reauthentication on a per-session basis while leveraging ZTF.

- **Why**: This solution is required to provide secure communications access to applications to support the organization's internal and external customers.

Use Case Components

The *what* statement should describe what service is being used and what products are involved, and provide a simple understanding of the service.

The *who* statement describes the users, devices, or systems that are included in the Use Case.

The *where* statement simply describes where access will be allowed from in terms of geography or a location category description that is meaningful to the organization.

The *how* statement provides descriptions for the methods of access, acceptable security parameters, and the performance requirements, and provides the SLA as needed.

The *when* statement is the descriptor for time and persistence. With ZTF, the expectation should be the least permissive security that is terminated on a session-by-session basis with reauthentication requirements for the next session. Security permissions will be based on the organizational security policy and the ZTF capabilities of the service being utilized for SASE.

The *why* statement should be a high-level summary of the reason why the access should be terminated when the reason is no longer valid. This should allow for automatic removal of access as the organization's reason for access ceases.

Policy design

Policy components must be broken into the MVP. The MVP should be the least prescriptive version of the policy, which is viable as an independent policy but minimalistic to be leveraged in combination with other policies as needed by the orchestration platform. Every SDN technology solution that includes but is not limited to SD-WAN and SASE should be designed in a modular fashion with extremely small policies that may be compounded on demand. The modular idea is that any one module should be able to be replaced or substituted on demand.

The base configuration of any SDN solution should be just that – a base on which to apply a policy. This is the opposite of more than 40 years of engineering education and industry best practices. It feels wrong to the most talented engineers. However, it will feel right as soon as they see it work correctly in production and they will become converts. This is something that we have seen in practice over the past few years. This behavior is like Gartner's Hype Cycle, where the individual's behavior matches that of what Gartner describes as the market behavior for any innovative technology.

As in SD-WAN, SASE services should be deployed with a hierarchical templated approach whereby the layers of the hierarchy provide a minimal policy at each layer to satisfy security, SLA, performance, and compliance goals. For instance, in an SD-WAN design, the hierarchical model starts with the most common site or application policy and if it is matched at that point, traffic is forwarded without further latency. With security, the hierarchy is reversed, causing a conflict in performance versus security. With ZTF, everything is blocked, so it eliminates the need to have conflicting policies driving latency as no traffic is forwarded until it meets all the policies. Therefore, the traffic can be forwarded with minimal latency impact.

An effective SASE policy is modular, least prescriptive in design, hierarchical in deployment, and comprehensive when orchestrated.

To summarize, the SASE use case design method reduces the complexity of SASE design by focusing on one use for one service at a time. Each use case should contribute to the overall SASE Service with an MVP policy design that allows for orchestration, automation, and AIOps.

In the next section, we will explain use case value propositions for SASE.

Case Value

The primary value proposition for the Use Case method is simplicity. When communicating with SASE stakeholders, there must be a common basis of understanding that must be a written and agreed-upon scope. Without a written Use Case, the SASE project may cause consequences that impact the organization. The written Use Case allows the project manager to bring all stakeholders together for design and implementation.

For the project manager, a collective understanding of the final project outcome is necessary for the achievement of the project. Often, project teams vary in skill, understanding, perspective, and the context in which they interpret the project scope. By designing the project with a series of Use Case documents, each team can focus on their specific subject matter expertise. By doing so, the proof of value materializes in the testing phase of the project as each use case is proved ready for production.

The security team gains specific insights into what exceptions are required and how compliance will be achieved. The security team can preapprove the design to reduce change control issues before implementation.

For the network team, they gain performance understandings that drive pricing impact but can be free to design to specification without fear of over or underbuilding the solution. This is a considerable time saver for the design team.

For the financial team, the performance and security requirements drive the costing, which releases the burden for extensive analysis of the solution. If the project is designed within budget constraints, then it may be approved. If the project is designed over budget, then the stakeholders may be presented with the option to reduce their requirements or allocate an additional budget to the project.

For key stakeholders, less effort is required due to the simple construction of the design through the Use Cases. Each use case may be approved, rejected, or tuned to produce the desired outcome in a modular fashion. The meeting time is reduced as each Use Case brings focus to one specific need at a time instead of discussing all areas of need at once.

For the end user, they become the beneficiary of the project's focus. For the first time in their career, the UX becomes king.

Summary

The concept of a Use Case for design is several thousands of years old. Increasingly, over the past 100 years, we have moved beyond the pursuit of perfection and into an age where humans believe perfection is possible. Perfection is not possible. The pursuit of perfection is where most of the good things in life happen. The pursuit of perfection in every aspect of your life is a journey where you are acting in the best interest of others while being selfless or altruistic. Designing for the UX is altruistic and deeply satisfying as it helps our fellow humans. This is a concept above profit that has proven to enhance profitability.

In the next chapter, *Chapter 15, SASE Design*, we will discuss how design for SASE leverages concepts in DevOps, security, SD-WAN, and the cloud and displaces legacy LAN/WAN design principles primarily due to disaggregation of the data plane and the control plane activity, which changes the paradigm. We will provide Design Overview, Theory, Function, Support, and discuss how to Communicate effectively.

15
SASE Design

Engineering success requires successfully executing a strategy through knowledgeable technical resources that are empowered and enabled to perform. Often, the organization relies on previously successful efforts to define the criteria for current or future success. The results of tactical execution that leverages past success creates variable results. Failure rates can average more than 50% of projects, even those that leverage professionally qualified teams.

Often, organizations launch a project due to pressure for success without a design that guarantees success. The project should be held in the planning stage until the design provides a 99.999% probability of success. The organization's financial well-being is at risk from poorly designed projects.

At the peak of **Enterprise Resource Planning (ERP)** software implementation, over 80% of ERP projects that invested over $ 500,000 USD into the project caused the catastrophic financial failure of the organization that the project was to benefit. Whole companies were bankrupted, restructured, shuttered, and had their stock prices destroyed over failed ERP projects. Many companies invested hundreds of millions of dollars into the project only to tell the project team to ensure success by leveraging the current method of success within the organization.

Forensic research showed that many of these ERP projects grew to more than 20 times the original cost estimates and all provided a negative **Return on Investment (ROI)**. Analysis showed that most organizations tried to implement ERP software that leveraged past success within their technology teams. The major issue was that the organization would buy the best software, hire the best consultants, and then proceed to do everything in the prescribed method for success within their organization.

Prescribing the design or deployment of modern technology with the old method of success equals failure. Imagine buying a new automated harvesting system in the multi-million-dollar range and then hiring 1,000 workers to manually harvest the crop to protect the new system from damage. What if a person were to lose their job because they were constantly late for their new job, due to the time it took to walk 10 miles while their new car is parked in their garage to prevent wear and tear on the tires? Another example could be if you were to hire a nuclear engineer to develop models for nuclear reactor safety but required that they perform all engineering calculations on paper instead of using computer systems. In each case, these examples provide failure to all parties by leveraging a previously successful model as opposed to learning a new way of achieving success.

The future of successful, secure communications is **Secure Access Service Edge (SASE)**. Successful implementation is based on a successful design. To achieve that success, each organization must learn new methods for success. This learning process is uncomfortable but necessary for success.

Designing for SASE leverages concepts in **DevOps**, **Security**, **SD-WAN**, and the **cloud**, and displaces legacy **LAN/WAN** design principles primarily due to disaggregation of **Data Plane** and **Control Plane** activity.

In this chapter, we will identify what is needed for successful SASE, explain how the design should support production, understand the functional model, design a solution with operational support in mind, and explain SASE design.

In this chapter, we will cover the following main topics:

- Design Overview – identify what is needed for successful SASE
- Design Theory – explain how the design should support production
- Design Function – understand the functional model
- Design Support – design a solution with operational support in mind
- Design Communication – explain SASE Design

Design Overview

Zero is the most appropriate starting place with SASE design. Leveraging a **ZTF**-based design allows all additional security services to increase in value as implemented. SASE can be implemented one service at a time as needed. Each service must leverage interlocking and supporting policies so that no one service defeats the overall design.

ZTF starts with zero, which means all ports and systems are blocked until the access policy is met. As each attribute passes each test of the policy, resources are unlocked for the device, user, or system to make use of. The design must allow additional generations of secure services to integrate without reducing security or performance benefits.

Many organizations will start implementation with SD-WAN as it provides a direct replacement for the previous site-to-site communication solutions such as routed MPLS, point-to-point IPSEC tunnels, and other legacy solutions. SD-WAN provides API solutions to integrate with ZTF. SD-WAN also allows you to integrate with IdAM, IAM, and MFA solutions. Please note that all three identity access management concepts may be the same solution, depending on the marketing of the software developer.

The culture of design in your organization needs to embody the DevOps culture. A DevOps or DevSecOps evangelist will preach the lifestyle change that allows an organization to rapidly deploy software changes in real time to pursue perfection one iteration at a time. A design that ignores this philosophy in favor of the previous model, which requires linear or vertical integration of each change in the environment over a planned project, will cause financial failures within that organization. Neither the market nor malicious entities will wait for the perfect project plan. The market buys at 85% of perfection, which is democratically proven through capitalist voting mechanisms such as the financial currency of your choice. Malicious entities work 24/7, 365 days a year, without a defined workday, and have never been known to schedule an attack on your employer within a change control window.

The correct design allows instant upgrades on-demand as soon as the software is available. These types of upgrades should be delivered within hours of release and installed within a 15-second window while the SASE Service is in production. To achieve this expectation, orchestration must be in production with a rapid rollback solution. Implementation should be 15 seconds globally; rolling back if there is an issue must only take 15 seconds globally as well.

SASE design is not network design or security design, nor is it application design. SASE design is a combination of all three with operational design embedded. This requires a new generation of design architects that do not exist. Once you can understand that the right skill is not available in the market, the opportunity remains that you must build the type of architect that you need. This person is developed more through the DevOps mindset than formal training. The SASE services that they must design have no formal training available at the time the design is required. Training in Agile, Scrum, and DevOps will help train the mindset, but extensive training will be counterproductive as the benefit of these new ways of thinking is to leverage intuition. Intuition cannot be trained – it must be supported and allowed to flourish in the wild. Intuition is not valued in corporate cultures because it does not produce predictable outcomes.

Where the market failed in previous attempts to standardize project methodology is in the belief that any science could be finite. Every day, we learn new facts that may be true at a point in time but false at a different point in time. At one point, we believed in fail open security then fail closed, and today Zero Trust. We believed in ZTF years ago but could not train enough engineers to leverage it, so the market decided it was an impossible goal. Today has not solved the issues we previously had.

Recruiters are sent to find skilled resources in technology that are less than a year old. The most qualified engineers, architects, and developers are those without formal training that, at one point in history, were called hacks or hackers. This was long before the current definition of a hacker. These are the people that learn through trial and error. They are not deterred by a lack of documentation or training. The type of person needed is not something that can be recruited; it must be built within the organization. The organization must give its talented people the ability to improvise and permission to fail. We want the failures to be small and the improvements to be big. We need to build a performance culture that rewards this type of behavior.

In summary, the design process requires a new way of thinking to allow the organization to achieve performance, security, and experience goals. In the next section, we will explain how the design should support production.

Design Theory

Production goals are exactly that, they are *goals*. Measuring finite, reportable metrics in production is always wrong as it produces the wrong organizational behavior. If you substitute the **User Experience (UX)** for previous methods of measurement, human behavior starts to align with the reason that performance was measured. The temptation is to measure and manage by all available metrics. This has consistently proven to produce the wrong human-based results. This is a good point to insert AIOps for the system or service to be managed, whereas the human is charged with positive UX.

Design theory for SASE has not been written at the time of authoring this book. Practitioners of SASE subscribe to ZTF mixed with DevOps concepts. In each case of successful SASE Service deployment, the separation between the data plane and the control plane is observed. Additional planes are identified based on perspective and the design of the services as provided by the developer or service provider. In each case, the management plane is called out for each service independently with little to no overlap. Overlap or integration is done via APIs and facilitated via the orchestration plane. In many services, a control and user plane separation is in effect.

For our purposes, we need to realize that plane separation allows for a modular design that provides for compliance needs. Modular design allows for both rapid integration and clear delineation for audit purposes. When only the data plane or only the user plane contains sensitive information and all other planes act in a utility fashion, compliance becomes a simple ongoing function of the operational model. This approach not only makes the audit simpler but also enables real-time compliance models.

In summary, an operations-based design that targets the UX as an indication of correct performance is the goal of **SASE Design Theory**.

In the next section, we will understand the functional model for SASE design.

Design Function

Each SASE Service independently has a functional model for design provided by the developer of that service. In the process of SASE design, each functional model must be laid out to compare functions for overlap. Integration mapping will be via API and that should allow the push/pull relationships between each service. The overlay of functionality requires a policy design that eliminates competition between features, functions, or attributes utilized by each service.

SASE functional design accounts for overlap between integrated services and remediates functional overlap that could impact performance or security. Historically, this has not been a requirement for technical architects as each system or service would run independently with little to no competition at a functional level. Often, in the SDN, SD-WAN, and SASE markets, the implemented solution has a 10-30% overlap in functionality, which causes negative interactions between systems. Competition for authority happens between two incompatible control plane, management plane, or orchestration plane solutions that are interlocking. This causes consequences that may be catastrophic for the organization in production.

Examples of negative interactions between systems are often found when installing two competing brands, such as vendor A for SD-WAN and vendor B for WAN acceleration. In this scenario, in production, the control plane technology for both systems performs correctly independently. When used together, vendors A and B's control plane technology, which are fundamentally different in terms of their technology or how their function is executed, compete for control of the network traffic. This type of control plane competition directly impacts the data plane, which has a major impact on the UX. Often, this behavior can shut down the network. Common SD-WAN design recommendations include configuring the WAN acceleration to transparent mode, which reduces benefits and the overall value the solution provides for the organization.

In conclusion, there must be a reconciliation of functionality between individual services integrated within the overall SASE Service. The best practice going forward will be a logical overlay design of each service that allows competing functions to be documented and a policy to be developed to allow each service to function in cooperation instead of competition.

In the next section, we will design a solution with operational support in mind.

Design Support

Support is someone else's job… or is it? The traditional separation of work function by skill set or subject matter expertise is the method for scaling services. Unfortunately, it has not worked for many years. The industry continues to leverage the non-functional model as it represents academic best practices to achieve a multiplier of results from the workforce within any organization. Interestingly, this is often referred to as the factory model. More interesting is that the factory model has moved to **Just-in-Time (JIT)** and will be moving to something that looks more like a three-dimensional print-on-demand where demanded. The challenge of leveraging the model to scale the industrial revolution is the gap between the 1760s and today. We are in the fourth generation, which we call Industry 4.0, and our staffing model leverages division of labor from more than 250 years ago.

All XOps models, where X can be substituted for your favorite version of operations, strive to achieve operational experiences that directly and positively contribute to UX. The design for any current or future solution must be designed to create positive UX and therefore must be designed around the operational support model. Positive operational support reduces the impact on downtime, performance, security, function, and mean time to repair the service. SASE services must leverage AIOps to improve on each of these areas of impact for the overall experience of end users, operators, and developers.

An example of clean operational models comes from an aircraft manufacturer that was producing some of the best engineering designs. The aircraft was designed well and functioned well but was extremely hard to maintain due to its design. This beautiful design cost the aircraft dearly in terms of hours of downtime as it had to be repaired or maintained. The manufacturer solved this problem by putting the engineers into an office with a full glass wall that had to watch the assembly of the aircraft all day while working. The message was received, and the design issue was resolved quickly. Now, that aircraft is one of the easiest to maintain in operations.

To summarize, operations-centered design is imperative for SASE success. In DevOps, the service being developed should have an equal focus on the operational support model so that it is easy to repair.

In the next section, we will explain how the design should support production.

Design Communication

To communicate the necessities of SASE Service Design, it is necessary to differentiate legacy and future solutions. That differentiation starts with the understanding that the SASE Service Design will require a combination of skills from all technology teams within the organization. Any team missing in this effort is at risk of their scope being blocked from all communications within the company as well as externally.

SASE design is the process by which the service for secure communications is created and validated, and the operational models are identified by all service functions. The design process is not a paper-based exercise alone. In the process of design, DevOps models are used to prove, pilot, test, revise, iterate, and operationalize a **Minimum Viable Product (MVP)**.

Summary

SASE design mixes SD-WAN, cybersecurity, and DevOps design techniques to create a solution that meets the organization's needs today by integrating multiple applications, security, and network communications solutions into a cohesive strategic SASE Service.

SD-WAN design focuses on disaggregating data and the control plane to create a secure communication forwarding solution. Cybersecurity design is based on ZTF, in which all resources are blocked by default, and only by correctly meeting the policy requirements is any access permitted by unlocking the resource in a step-by-step fashion. DevOps places the operational support model at the heart of the solution, allowing for real-time updates to software at any time. Blending these models allows for a future-focused solution that is as easy to maintain as possible.

Design theory will continue to evolve. Leveraging a philosophy around DevOps with a grounding in ZTF brings you closer to this. An SDN mechanism to leverage all paths that are available instantly when they become available rounds out the picture. When the theory is written, realize that it will be just a model for education and not a prescription for success.

Functional design helps the human element understand overlapping functions that must be cared for; otherwise, the service will be impacted negatively. Overlaying the model in design software creates a solid visualization of functions that may negatively compete. The policy must be designed to account for the attributes in each function as somewhat of a tiebreaker to eliminate the competition and ensure successful experiences.

Communicating the value of SASE design involves teaching a new perspective to those who have successfully leveraged the previous perspective to this point in their career.

SASE design is a live interaction with the solution that must be evergreen for success.

In the next chapter, *Chapter 16, SASE Trust*, we will discuss a cybersecurity architecture where all **actors** are authenticated, authorized, and continuously validated before **subjects** are granted access to, maintain access to, or perform operations on **targets**.

16
SASE Trust

In SASE, there is no trust! SASE has been identified as an evolutionary, secure communications service. It is based on a collection of existing services. The standards being developed for SASE are providing a revolutionary improvement in how secure communications are achieved. Every few weeks, SASE evolves through the DevOps process. In production, the foundation for effective SASE is a **Zero Trust Framework** (**ZTF**).

With the ZTF, all resources, systems, communications, and so on are closed by default, and only by successfully meeting security policy requirements are resources unlocked. Imagine network cards that only receive electrical signaling once all policy requirements are met. In the ZTF, switch ports would require active **Multi-Factor Authentication** (**MFA**) approval prior to allowing a specific network card to receive any access to the port. There are potentially hundreds of layers of security that can be employed through the ZTF, and all those security controls can now be processed in a few milliseconds. Both maintenance and support of this complex solution can be automated through AIOps solutions.

In this chapter, we will discuss how to live without trust, a cybersecurity architecture where all actors are authenticated, authorized, and continuously validated before subjects are granted access to, maintain access to, or perform operations on targets.

We will cover the following main topics in this chapter:

- Zero Overview – understand high level Zero Trust Framework
- Zero Framework – detail out the framework model
- Zero Feed – feed the framework with the needed functions
- Zero Trust – trust the solution through understanding
- Zero Explained – explain ZTF to stakeholders

Zero Overview

Firewall-based solutions have had mixed success over the years. What is called a next-generation firewall today is simply a suite of security applications running on a system that was designed to block network traffic. Each time you read the words *block network traffic*, it should become more painful and confusing. Blocking network traffic implies layer three communications or, more specifically traffic, on just one layer, the network. The issue with blocking network traffic is the fact that our attack surface is across all layers of the **Open Systems Interconnection** (**OSI**) model, across every protocol. For this reason, firewalls are not effective protection against almost any threat. The effectiveness of firewall services on the market is based on the additional services or features they build into or around the actual firewall service.

A new model had to be created. Previous attempts to solve security issues have had limited traction on the market, due to skill, cost, and limited effectiveness. To attempt to get ahead of the threat, the ZTF was born.

Many organizations rely on **Zero Trust Network Access** (**ZTNA**) as their zero-trust solution; however, ZTNA is a product that can leverage the ZTF but is not the ZTF. ZTNA is a product that replaces remote-access VPN solutions. The ZTF is the framework by which ZTNA may be effective when deployed correctly. There is no ZTF product or service available to purchase. Be wary of one-stop solutions in this market space.

A deeper dive into **Zero Trust Architecture** (**ZTA**) is provided in *NIST SP 800-207 – Zero Trust Architecture*: `https://csrc.nist.gov/publications/detail/sp/800-207/final`.

The MEF Forum actively works to define a ZTF standard with their *Zero Trust Framework and Service Attributes* (MEF W118) working group. Both efforts are attempting to make the concept of zero trust achievable through clearly defined standards.

In summary, the principles ZTF include an organized and necessarily ruthless approach to secure communications safely.

In the next section, we will detail the framework model.

Zero Framework

The initial components of the ZTF are IAM, access control, policy management, policy enforcement, and monitoring of all components. The ZTF does nothing by itself and only provides value when leveraged in conjunction with SASE services. These are dependent upon the ZTF components to continually provide effective security. Eventually, most SASE services will eliminate overlapping solution components. However, it is not expected that all attribute overlap will be removed. The reason some services must overlap features, functions, attributes, and other components is context. Context is the most often misunderstood concept when providing any human or machine communication. We will cover context in the upcoming *Zero trust* section.

Zero trust leverages the foundational concepts of the validated identity of the user, device, system, service, resource, or application, prior to any policy that allows access.

Identity is the first and highest priority. If we can eliminate anyone or anything that should not have access, then we are able to eliminate front-door security access issues. Effective systems for validating a user, device, or systems are a prerequisite to building any modern service.

Policy is at the heart of all software-defined solutions on the market. An effective policy should be least permissive and least prescriptive. Developing policies that are small, independent, and simple modules allows both orchestration and automation to achieve desired compound effects on-demand as determined by the software management and control policies. It is not possible to write one policy that accounts for every possible variation in needs. Light policies can be leveraged through orchestration to build hierarchical models that an automation platform can mix and match to achieve desired outcomes. The more beautiful, perfect, or complex a policy is when designed, the more quickly it will fail in production.

Enforcement ensures that the design of a policy is put into use. The effectiveness of enforcement relies on and correlates directly to the policy. Firewalls provide a linear concept to understand enforcement as a gate that is open or closed. Actual enforcement should have a creative license to leverage any tool available in an SASE service. An example of this would be an intrusion prevention system that runs automated scripts with permission to block, allow, mitigate, isolate, shunt, return, attack, or ignore malicious traffic inflight without human intervention. None of these options are available without design, testing, authorization, pre-approved change in production, libraries of scripts, and an effective policy.

Monitoring is required to ensure that the desired behavior is occurring. It is not enough to design or implement an effective solution. Much like teaching children, it is imperative to monitor real-life actions, which allows for reward, mitigation, discipline, and improvement. The monitoring process provides real-world feedback on how effective execution has been up to this point. Neither politics nor emotions should factor into the feedback. Observe and then take action to achieve the desired result.

Continual improvement, takes the output of monitoring systems as input for analysis to continually refine the entire framework. This manifests as the intended CI/CD processes that are taught in DevOps. The feedback from the monitoring solution is necessary to understand where improvement is needed. Effective teams will leverage this input relentlessly to achieve success for their organization. More money, time, labor, and resources should be placed into continual improvement efforts than any other investment. The investments at this point in the process are sunk costs. The initial ROI has been spent.

Much like a rose garden, the perpetual investments made after planting achieves the most beautiful results.

In summary, the ZTF is a framework for security success built upon identity, policy, enforcement, monitoring, and improvement. Improvement that can also be iterative development provides a critical ROI.

In the next section, we will feed the framework needed functions.

Zero Feed

If the baseline is zero, then value must be added to the solution to achieve desired outcomes. Think of as an equation with an intial zero value; each positive integer applied increases the equation's final value such as zero plus one equals one. With ZTF on your network, no device, system, or application provides any value since all access to all resources are explicitly denied. Value of the device, system, or application is only achieved by policies allowing approved communications.

The inherent value is security for SASE, but the benefit to an organization is realized through effective communications across all users, resources, and devices, required to enable the organization to serve its purpose. Starting from zero, and then adding the required functionality for success, provides the proper care and feeding for the ZTF to provide its value to the organization.

Effective human intelligence requires information from as many sources as possible in order to evaluate trends that are either positive or negative. Effective secure communications services also require as many sources or feeds as possible. The more feeds into a system for analysis, the more accurate the output.

With any SASE service, such as SD-WAN, the first step is use case design. Once use cases have a design, the next step is to create an inventory of the services required to fulfill the goal described in the use case. In our SD-WAN instance, it will require IAM, orchestration, monitoring, DNS, DHCP, AIOps, API integration, and other external systems to both enable the secure provisioning of services and maintain security in production.

As we enable each external component to integrate with and interact with the SD-WAN service, we lay the groundwork for the feedback necessary for security intervention. Most legacy security solutions are independent, which allows significant room for exploitation. SASE and the ZTF require an active approach to security, integrating input from all available services to create a least permissive access environment by analyzing all sources for policy compliance. The key to success is policies that account for input received about the decisions that are made to allow access. With the ZTF, it is not about blocking access; it is about allowing access because all access is blocked by default.

Feed the ZTF all available information sources to allow the policy to interact with changing conditions of all types. The SASE service needs a policy to define parameters where access is acceptable, and outside those parameters, all access is blocked by default. Continual monitoring is a required service function to constantly feed into the framework all the known activity for the application of policy.

In conclusion, the ZTF needs the input feeds from as many adjacent services as possible to make the best possible decisions in compliance with the policy.

In the next section, we will trust the solution through understanding.

Zero Trust

As an end user, it is convenient to trust your laptop, specific people, and specific software applications. Much of the issues with security for any organization, whether physical or logical, comes from someone trusting. Security issues are often caused by accidents; it's like leaving a gate open and letting a pet out. With the pet, it may not make sense to do a double gate system, whereby one gate has to be closed to open the other. With technology, we need to employ security far more effectively than two gates; we need both defaults to closed and fails closed.

Sessions in zero trust, once authorized, are trusted until they are terminated. Any new session between a subject and target actors must be reauthorized prior to passing either control or data plane traffic. In the future, life cycle sessions may monitor a session for indications of extraordinary behavior such as gross variations in throughput or quality. The life cycle session would have the ability to remediate malicious activity without impact on the session or UX.

Context is often misunderstood in human conversation. In the ZTF, context is both required and relevant for security. If the context by which authorization was approved changes, the session may be terminated. A change in context may not directly represent a threat, but statistical sessions are singular in context, and the change represents statistical anomalies that must be investigated. In addition to terminating the session after a change in context, the security operations team or AIOps tool should create an incident for forensic analysis.

To summarize, the ZTF solves the issue of trust by not allowing anyone to trust anyone or anything.

In the next section, we will explain the ZTF to stakeholders.

Zero Explained

The best way to explain the ZTF is by stating that access to every user, device, system, or system component is locked out by a default policy, and each component is unlocked by meeting the policy requirements for access one at a time. Essentially, if zero trust works correctly, then nothing works unless an explicit policy match is achieved.

It is necessary that the ZTF be aggressive to ensure that an organization is as safe as possible. The ZTF replaces standard firewall concepts by working through all layers of the **Open Systems Interconnection (OSI)** model. It accounts for what is happening in the world as opposed to what is expected to happen in the world. All security services will leverage the ZTF as the standard going forward.

To explain the effort required for the ZTF is to explain the benefit of uninterrupted execution of an organization's mission. The ZTF is the method of eliminating the impact of a cyberattack on the organization.

The ZTF is the framework where effective security is accomplished by only allowing access to that which has been verified and authorized access to each resource required.

Summary

On the market, many services offer reasonable levels of cybersecurity. Is reasonable a good enough standard for your organization? Is it worth the effort to be perpetually vigilant with an ever-evolving security model? Is it reasonable to expect your experts to be constantly learning new methods to ensure that your organization is safe from attack? Ultimately, you are the person that answers these questions with what you do with the information you have received so far in your journey. Is it worth the effort to out-evolve the threat?

Zero trust is a philosophy to approach secure communications. It requires diligence in execution that is aided through perpetual learning, perpetual monitoring, and perpetual adaptation of policy.

In the next chapter, we will outline a new model for learning. SASE is a moving target that will not stop evolving. How do you learn something that is perpetually becoming more complex daily? How do you get ahead of the requirements? Where can you independently research this subject?

Part 4 – SASE Bonus Perspective

Part 4 offers bonus material to achieve success. SASE requires a new perspective, a new way of learning, a new way of designing, a new way of carrying out the code release process, and a new way of thinking about change. This part of the book introduces the key concepts for success beyond technology.

In this section, there are the following chapters:

- *Chapter 17, SASE Learn*
- *Chapter 18, SASE DevOps*
- *Chapter 19, SASE Forward*
- *Chapter 20, SASE Bonus*

17
SASE Learn

SASE is a moving target that will not stop evolving. How do you learn something that is perpetually becoming more complex daily? How do you get ahead of the requirements? Where can you independently research this subject?

SASE is *THE* new standard for secure communications. It does not follow the pattern for previous technical implementation, thereby making previous skills irrelevant to the conversation. In the past, all technology was a mathematical improvement on previous generations of technology. Any improvement can be taught as an incremental supplement education to the existing curriculum available in the market. SASE, SD-WAN, and Zero Trust models are not incremental changes to the previous solutions. They are not subject to the rules and the developer has creative license to innovate as their solutions are divorced from the hardware requirements. This is achieved through abstraction such as the use of a hypervisor that normalizes behavior for the hardware. The freedom to create any new model of solving a problem with SASE is available to the developer as they see fit.

The market for SASE or other **Software Defined Networking** (**SDN**) solutions is evolving a generational life cycle at the pace of three Scrum Sprint Cycles, which can range from 2 to 6 weeks depending on the company and the software. The tangible impact on engineering teams is that the product or service installed can become a completely different product in 6 to 18 weeks. This impacts training and requires a just-in-time model that re-educates engineering teams at approximately 6-week increments throughout the year.

With abstraction solving the issue of legacy needs for the hardware to properly support the software goals, the developer is no longer bound to a specific model. The freedom to design software without rules has caused an educational gap whereby those who learn independently through trial and error are undeterred, and those who rely on traditional learning models are left behind as the market can take 3 years to develop a curriculum for new technology and by that point, it is irrelevant because the market has released several generations of software-based, software-defined solutions.

A new model for learning is required! The new model must be modular and flexible to allow engineering teams the ability to make education something they do daily with an evolutionary learning cycle that matches the Sprint Cycle utilized by their software vendors.

In this chapter, we will learn about identifying how to learn SASE, developing a new learning model, understanding the new modality of the model, identifying when to leverage the learning model, and explaining the new learning model to others.

We will cover the following main topics in this chapter:

- Learn Overview – identify how to learn SASE
- Learn Model – develop a new learning model
- Learn Perpetual – understand the new modality of the model
- Learn Timing – identify when to leverage the learning model
- Learn Explain – explain the new learning model

Learn Overview

Throughout history, technological innovations have been treated with disdain and violence. It is often felt that innovation causes winners and losers, which in turn causes strife. Many wars throughout history have been related to the changes caused by technical advances in society. Fear and anxiety come from change, which often has led to inaction. This inaction has been detrimental and often deadly. Each time a major societal change occurs, the early adopters benefit in a disproportionate measure from the mid- and late adopters. For this reason, the people that can spot a trend in the initial stages and then take positive action become the winners. Those who fight the change while lagging become the losers. Those who follow the trend without lagging benefit in many ways by consuming what the winner has achieved.

The purpose of this chapter is to enable you to join the winners in embracing the change in trend from physically defined to software-defined, secure communications services. In fact, this learning model can and should be applied to every area of life for maximum benefit in this ever-changing world.

In the early days of personal computers, those who learned by doing before the user manual was created were called hackers. Today, we attach a stigma to the term *hacker*. The common belief is that a hacker is a person that has malicious intent and is trying to either steal from or harm someone. Interestingly, the term *hack* means different things to diverse types of people. In the early days of computing, the hacker was just someone figuring out how things work by trial and error. In sports or writing, it is a derogatory term for someone that does not do an excellent job. Professional drivers often spend years pursuing a *Hack License* that allows them to earn a professional level of income in their profession. In the taxicab driver profession, the term originates from the Hackney borough in London, England, after which the Hackney carriages were named and eventually called a hack. In the context of this discussion, a hacker is a person that learns by trial and error how to use a new product.

The spirit of the hacker is one by which a person faced with an undocumented or under-documented product or service will work independently or collaboratively to learn how to utilize it. The trial and error, self-discovery, and hacking methods of learning are actively taught against in schools globally.

The market is producing needed technology solutions to current problems at such an aggressive pace that educational systems have little chance to address the educational need. A new learning solution is required.

Technical education is required that can meet the market demand with availability within six weeks of any new software release that materially changes the way any specific technology works in the market. The market is not currently equipped for this issue in either a traditional academic setting or a corporate learning environment.

The solution to almost every issue within any society can be education and the most effective solution for societal issues is perpetual education. This has been discussed since the Renaissance period in world history and in every ancient civilization. Unfortunately, most cultures throughout history sought to solve this problem for their top class or caste with little benefit for the general population. The solution is perpetual learning. Modern social systems generally handle education as a gate-keeping system for earned achievement models. The issue with this approach is that it both serves a limited number of people and is considered an event or an achievement. If learning is an achievement or an event, then it occurs once and then the human that completes their educational journey either stops learning or learns at an ineffective pace for the rest of their life. If education becomes a systematic approach to life whereby each human seeks to learn daily, then it becomes perpetual. Each person can learn at a comfortable pace that outpaces entertainment in their life. That is, the value of learning in this model is a perpetual and iterative achievement. The reward for achievement outweighs the distraction of entertainment. This approach allows a person to evolve intellectually, and perpetually, which creates a utopian model for lifetime achievement that is redefined perpetually in that human mind. The concept of utopia is that of a perfect world. Unfortunately, there is no perfection at rest because everything decays naturally. However, perfection through progress is a worthwhile pursuit because the byproducts of improvement benefit all humans touched by that pursuit. There is no human problem that cannot be solved with education and the application of that education.

In summary, education must be redefined into an executed model for perpetual lifetime learning.

In the next section, we will develop that new learning model.

Learn Model

At this point in the book, it has become apparent that the intentional violation of literary convention has been executed to cause an emotional reaction to and connection with the content of this book. This was a required tool for helping you specifically to benefit from this book, which will become more apparent by the third time you read this book. The idea that we would use the *Learn Model* title for this section should have created a question that we will hopefully answer for you here.

Success in education is achieved when the knowledge gained by the educational process is utilized successfully with a positive return on investment in the real-world application of that knowledge. To help you, you must create a model that works for you to learn. The proof that the model you created works is in a real-world application. The report card mechanism is often *pass* or *fail* when you execute a solution based on the knowledge you acquired utilizing the model you created. The mathematical score applied to the pass or fail becomes a quality standard to grade the level of success, allowing you to show improvement the next time you execute that knowledge in application. The bottom line is to model, learn, execute, evaluate, and repeat.

My learning model is based on the concept of a *Book of Lists* that contains all the known and unknown knowledge on a particular project. I use a Microsoft Excel workbook or a new paper notebook to start the process. I write an idea of what I want to achieve and then write out everything I know about the idea in categories. For example, if I wanted to create a new flavor of ice cream, I would write out the overall idea as a starting place and then I would go through the notebook, naming each page as a category. With Excel, I create spreadsheet tabs, one per category, and I would save the filename as `new.flavor.Ice.Cream.1.0`.

Here is a *Book of Lists* example:

Idea: Create a new flavor of ice cream

Categories of knowledge:

- Common flavors
- Common ingredients
- Common process
- Interesting names
- Potential ingredients
- Potential process improvements
- Marketing plan
- Who could provide feedback?
- Subject Matter Experts that I know
- Who to research?
- Why ice cream?
- History of ice cream
- Questions and answers
- Research sources
- Costs
- Equipment required
- Regulatory requirements
- Restrictions

Important to note is not how thorough my ice cream lists are but that I started learning by writing what I could think of in the order I thought of it. The first place to start from is step 0 but many people never start because they want to follow the steps in order. A hacker does not know the order because they were not formally trained, and neither should you. Learning is a beautiful process that expands the mind. It cannot be defined by boundaries because every human is different. I do not expect you to follow my process exactly because it is not a recipe. I will not give you a recipe because what works for me will not work for you as your brain is uniquely designed to function in a way that benefits you. For this reason, you must create your own model. Please feel free to try mine and modify it as quickly as you wish.

Once I create the tabs or pages for the categories, I go to each and write down everything I know in short statements. For me, I may summarize a concept in a single word that triggers a comprehensive thought, I may write a paragraph or two for each thought, or I may just create bullet points for each thought. The purpose is to trigger inverse thoughts about what I do not know in the form of questions. I document all the questions that I would like answers to on a separate tab or page. When I am done documenting everything I can think of, I start researching on the internet to get quick answers that should be 70-80% accurate as it helps me quickly gain knowledge. Prior to the execution of my project, I will validate all required data with 99% accuracy. The quick wins in progress create momentum that accelerates the process, and data that is 85% accurate but obtained in minutes is preferred to data at 100% accuracy that takes months. The overall goal is to try and fail as many times as needed to get to the win.

The next item needed is a high-level outline of a project plan. Learning without execution causes a dilution of knowledge at rest. In other words, learning without action, and learning without testing, provides little to no benefit to the world.

A simple, high-level, project plan would look like this:

1. Identify idea or concept.
2. Create a book of lists.
3. Start research.
4. Develop **Proof of Concept (POC)/Proof of Value (POV)**.
5. Test and evaluate.
6. Pilot 1-10% of production scale completion.
7. Test and evaluate.
8. Implement into production to approximately 95% completion.
9. Remediate the approximately 5% that failed.
10. Start over for iteration 2.0, which must be a generational improvement on *steps 1-9*.
11. Start over for iteration 3.0, which must be a generational improvement on *steps 1-9*.
12. Start over for iteration 4.0, which must be a generational improvement on *steps 1-9*.

The first lesson is to use the POC/POV and Pilot processes to reduce the cost of failure.

The second lesson is that iterative and generational improvement offers greater value each time than the original idea in production.

In summary, the model must be unique for you or your organizational culture, but it cannot be based on something you learned in college. It must be a new creation that is continually validated, continually proven, and evolves through iteration.

In the next section, we attempt to understand the modality of the model.

Learn Perpetual

Modality is an interesting concept when leveraging written language as we do not have the context or human expression available to assist in our understanding of what the writer is trying to convey. Modality could be in the category of *possibility, deduction, expectation, permission, obligation, ability,* or *habit*:

- **Possibility** defines something that theoretically is possible. Perpetual motion is theoretically impossible and, therefore, human nature is to dismiss that anything could obtain perpetuity. Possibility is also the hope of humanity and the catalyst for attempting to achieve the theoretical impossibility.

- **Deduction** causes unnecessary delay in action through excessively cautious analysis. Deduction can be leveraged to improve the probability of successful outcomes when placed in a secondary position to the accomplishment of the mission.

- **Expectation** in this case implies failure as the natural outcome of trying something new. Expectation may be leveraged to visualize a positive outcome that encourages the accomplishment of a goal.

- **Permission** to try a new way of learning is not a prerequisite for learning or its attempt. Permission to achieve should be first granted internally within one's own mind prior to any concept of external permission.

- **Obligation** often causes a person to dismiss the possibility of achievement as the two are often considered incompatible cooperative engagements. Obligation to one's own responsibilities is often the fuel that stokes the creative fires to achieve a desirable outcome.

- **Ability** or **inability** is a negotiable concept and not required at the start of the learning process. Ability is inherent in the mind of those who will not quit no matter how much is required for success.

- **Habit** is the predetermined mechanism for failure. Habit can also be leveraged to create positive systematic change in the individual, which becomes contagious for the organization.

Modality can be both the conduit for positive change and the excuse to avoid positive change. Modality is just methodology, and the method can be leveraged for both positive and negative outcomes.

In conclusion, the modality in every context must be perpetual learning for your benefit, your organization's benefit, and the benefit of those you care about.

In the next section, we identify when to leverage the learning model.

Learn Timing

Leveraging the five W's is always a wonderful place to start with any learning model. The five W's for those who are unfamiliar are *Who*, *What*, *Why*, *Where*, and *When*. We often unofficially add a qualifier of *How* or *How much* to the mix, but it does not start with W and, therefore, is left out sometimes. In this section, we talk about *when*. The correct answer is *always*! *The timeline is within six weeks of every relevant software release.*

Over time, as your new learning model becomes more familiar to you, it can be applied to any area of your life or organization. Initially, leverage the model when attempting to use an innovative technology that is either undocumented, under-documented, or has inadequate training available. This model is to create a way of learning something without the necessary training program available for success.

Timing in this case stands for just-in-time. There is an entire logistical science for just-in-time logistics. The scientific approach attempts to deliver what is needed when needed and not days prior to the need. This approach reduces inventory costs, which can exceed net profit within some industries causing systemic failure. This approach also backfires with supply chain disruptions such as natural disasters. Many logistical systems only have a 72-hour reserve built in. If the consumer panics by over-purchasing in any one category, the system fails the next consumer for up to three days. If a natural disaster occurs, the reserve is naturally depleted while awaiting normal service conditions.

Just-in-time education for software is relegated to release notes, existing white papers, and data sheets that were developed prior to release. Formal, corporate training lags the market by an average of 36 months, while formal academic training on the same subject may be delayed up to eight years prior to incorporation into collegiate education. While reasonable approaches to education may justify the delay, the market is both relentless and unforgiving of these gaps. It is common for the market to pay a 10x multiplier for labor in innovative software deployments due to the skill gaps. The sources of the labor that know their worth are those who taught themselves informally to the benefit of their employer and their customers, either internal or external.

To summarize, just-in-time training has always been used but is often treated in a derogatory manner, which serves to discourage classically trained talent from its practice.

In the next section, we learn how to explain the new learning model to others.

Learn Explain

The new learning model is a self-taught approach by which engineering talent is promoted and rewarded for perpetually learning in alignment with and ahead of organizational needs.

The model is a combination of just-in-time, trial and error, testing, self-education, and perpetual learning. It requires that the student and the teacher be the same person without a curriculum to learn from. The timeline for proficiency is within six weeks every time the product or service evolves.

When explaining the need, it is important to clarify that formal education will not be available until after the product is scheduled for removal from production because the speed of the market in response to security concerns requires immediate updates on demand.

Software development cycles necessitate a 6- to 18-week goal for learning any new product or service. There are no subject matter experts to leverage until after it is too late for the organization to benefit from the new product or service. The whole organization must learn to adapt to the speed of the market.

Missing security functionality can cause bankruptcy and criminal charges for organizations that do not make this change.

Summary

In the future, software systems will incorporate education within each software release making this approach to education feel more systematic and normal. Successful organizations will develop their own model for perpetual learning prior to that point in the market.

A perpetual, just-in-time approach to technology education is required for organizational viability. This model does not exist, and it is up to each of us to develop a way of achieving the mission of our organization prior to a permanent solution.

More information on SASE education can be found at each manufacturer, developer, service provider, and standards organization. Follow-on education is available at `Mef.net` under the **SASE** topic.

In the next chapter, *SASE DevOps*, we will learn how to understand DevOps as a model and how it relates to SASE, understand the *fervor* of the DevOps mindset, continual integration, and when and how to act on information, and explain the impact of DevOps on SASE.

18
SASE DevOps

DevOps plays a significant role in SASE as a doctrinal practice to ensure security throughout the software development life cycle. The primary differences between legacy software development practice and DevOps are a focus on **Continuous Integration/Continual Delivery (CI/CD)** and the integration of the operations component. Instead of developing software and handing it off to someone else to operate it, the DevOps team develops with the operations team as their key customer. It is more common today for a software support team and the software development team to be one comprehensive team. That one team performs all processes from cradle to grave for the application that they are responsible for.

SASE DevOps is realized when purchasing SASE services from a service provider that is also the developer and the operator of those services. Occasionally, the model involves all contributors being from one company or organization. More commonly, the contributors to the DevOps team for a specific SASE service are multi-skilled and cross-functional contributors from multiple organizations that contribute to the development, operations, and optimization components of the DevOps cycle. This is more frequently the case when leveraging open source products, as often the end user is not the creator but must contribute code and tools for successful operations of the product.

We have arrived at the age of open collaboration where successful organizations study each other's code to collectively make the world better. Competing concepts that have slowed market progress include the perceived benefits of securing **Intellectual Property (IP)**, the perceived liabilities of sharing code, the perceived security risks of using open code, and most commonly, *fear*. In the past few years, we have seen every major corporation leverage some open products as well as most governments. With the mainstream use of open products, security has increased through investments made. Some organizations have committed to only using open products and have hired qualified DevOps resources to ensure performance, security, and end user experience. Many of these organizations have assigned thousands of workers to these open projects. While the future may not be exclusively open, the collaboration required for effective DevOps practice drives teams to function across multiple internal and external teams for every effective project.

In this chapter, we will learn to understand DevOps as a model and how it relates to SASE, understand the *fervor* of the DevOps mindset, continual improvement, and when and how to act on information, and explain the impact of DevOps on SASE.

We will cover the following main topics in this chapter:

- DevOps Overview – understand DevOps as a model and how it relates to SASE
- DevOps Fervor – understand the fervor of the DevOps mindset
- DevOps Continuous – understand continual improvement
- DevOps Act – understand how to act on information
- DevOps Impact – explain the impact of DevOps on SASE

DevOps Overview

From a high level, DevOps looks like an infinite loop where by following the workflow, each cycle finishes, allowing the next cycle to start. The loop does not have a start or end because a team may take over work at any step in the cycle. Occasionally, a team member may specialize in one step in the process, but the most effective teams are cross-functional and multi-skilled.

The effective DevOps project manager may also be a great **Information Technology Infrastructure Library** (**ITIL**) practitioner. The best developer may also have an affinity for tool creation. The key support technician may have the best pre-deployment testing skills. All team members are expected to both support end users as well as invest in the feedback loop. In today's technology environment, vertical specialists have become a liability due to software development life cycles, which are in 2-to-6-week increments as well as achieving obsolescence within 18 to 36 weeks.

The **Return on Investment** (**ROI**) on educating a singularly skilled resource to perform a single function no longer exists. This issue is like comparing Industry 1.0 to Industry 4.0 workers. In 4.0, a worker must be able to repair the machine they are working with, in both physical and software-based systems, as well as operate the machine and perform basic network troubleshooting to ensure all system components can communicate. The 1.0 manufacturing worker only had to repeat a single function for the production system to function. In 1.0, a worker may only cut a single part of a shoe hundreds of times per day for years. In 4.0, the worker may have to learn new software features weekly to guarantee zero variance in the cutting process for the same shoe their grandparent was cutting manually.

DevOps charts demonstrating the steps in the process vary from organization to organization but can be summarized as *plan*, *code*, *build*, *test*, *release*, *operate*, and *monitor*. It is recommended that CI/CD, notify, and act become canonized, as they embody the spirit of the DevOps mindset. Consistently including these steps allows for iteration and life cycle improvements. Throughout all the steps in the process, innovation, improvement, refinement, and communications are encouraged. Each step requires action on the part of the person or system that notices action is necessary.

There have been several billionaires caught picking up trash, which is obviously not their job. The point is that the trash indicated an issue. The leadership lesson is that nobody is too important that they cannot act when necessary to improve an environment for the whole organization. If you see a problem, act at your skill level. If you do not have the skill to fix a specific problem, then notify someone that does have the skill. Do not treat any problem as beneath you or your position. Many organizations have failed in their mission as well as financially because individuals within the organization ignored the problems they noticed.

Included in the following subsection is an example outline to communicate with your team what high-level steps are included in a DevOps practice that focuses on SASE services.

SASE DevOps

So, let's get started with the high-level steps:

1. **Plan**: Plan the product based on all available requirements and any feedback from prior iterations of the same product or similar use cases.
2. **Code**: Code the components of the solution into **Minimum Viable Product** (**MVP**) modules that can be assembled in different orders to achieve different results. The MVP should be as small of a module as possible to allow for integration as needed by the policy engine, as well as the AIOps solution.
3. **Build**: Build a working product or service.
4. **Test**: Test each module's function as well as the comprehensive solution. Validate performance, **User Experience** (**UX**), and security.
5. **Release**: Release the product into production with a goal of no more than 15 packets lost in the transition from the previous product or service. This requires active change during the production day. If the product is expected to cause a loss of more than 15 packets during the transition to production, demote the package for additional testing until the expectations are met.
6. **CI/CD**: CI/CD should be lifestyle choices for success. Executing an MVP distribution and improving through iteration while redeploying constantly allows for the value of the product to continually increase while providing improved UX. Integration with adjacent systems allows for increased value to the feedback loop.
7. **Operate**: Operate as though the product was the key income producer for the organization because, often, the simple product that has no ties to financial outcomes is the one that drives away revenue through a negative impact on customers.
8. **Monitor**: Monitor through a continuous feedback loop to inspect what you expect.
9. **Notify**: Notify security teams, operations teams, workflow management, end users, and customer systems as often as possible.
10. **Action**: Action is required as close to an event, issue, or variation as possible to ensure UX.
11. **Start over at step one (1) with iteration**: Start over at 1 with iteration. The DevOps process is effective through iteration.

In summary, DevOps is the devout, fervent application of systems that provide neither operation nor development of systems independently but both development and operations with continual improvement.

In the next section, we will try to understand the fervor of the DevOps mindset.

DevOps Fervor

A practice that we place the utmost importance on, to the point where it becomes a core part of our personal and community culture, is also one that is intimately and sometimes violently protected. For example, today many people aggressively pursue personal health more than anything else in their life. Many people protect their personal beliefs at any cost. There are many forms of government whereby the key members become fervent in their approach to ensure as many people convert to their concept of political perfection. Most of us go through phases in life where we can both understand and relate to many different belief systems.

Fervor is an intense passion for a concept, person, place, or thing. Devout is someone who faithfully executes their belief system. A splendid example of a practitioner is someone who practices what they believe in their daily life.

Devout DevOps practitioners execute their belief in the DevOps model with a fervor that can be overwhelming to outsiders. This can cause those who do not understand DevOps to avoid the practice and its practitioners in daily life. Be assured that their fervor is beneficial to your organization. Their methods will cause positive progress in security as well as the performance of everything they touch. Their fervor will enable your organization to break through the barriers in place due to legacy security and software development models. In fact, their highest aspiration is DevSecOps as an integrated practice for all software development and the operational support model for any software in production for your organization. Once you understand their culture better, you will find yourself helping to convert the masses to a better way of thinking.

One key thing to understand about their culture is that current software is not secure, as it was not intended to operate in the open world. It was intended to operate behind a firewall, and in the future, we will need every packet transmitted in communications to go over public networks and house its own firewall equivalent system. Can we put a firewall in a packet? No, the firewall code is cumbersome and will not fit in a few bytes; however, we can develop secure communications with SASE and zero trust that provide security built into every packet. SASE, SSE, and similar concepts will eliminate the need for any private network, thereby allowing every device to access the internet by whatever means available to the device. Secure communications leveraging a **Zero Trust Framework** (**ZTF**) will allow any user to use any device over any connection method safely, all the time, and as the policy allows.

The fervor of the DevOps practitioner will encourage you to work through challenges on the path to integrating a ZTF in all systems. We need these humans to have a devout approach to their craft so that they can persist where others have failed to divorce and remove legacy code, which provides an attack surface for those with malicious intentions. It is a hard job to work through billions of lines of legacy code to find a function and recreate it in an entirely secure model. Success is only available to those who gain the correct level of executive support within their organization, as this takes the world's two most valuable resources – time and money. You can support the DevOps mindset within your organization to achieve effective, secure solutions that are based on the ZTF.

A tough-to-live-with example of where that fervor will come in handy is the change control window within your organization. Change control windows must be eliminated. Change control must become a real-time continual deployment model. Do not deploy into an offline, out-of-production, change window, as this will skew test results and make your organization weaker. The threats to any organization must be eliminated in real time. The primary risk of attack today is the time between when a vulnerability starts to exist and when the solution to mitigate it is in production. The time you notice a problem is not the time to fix it. The correct time to fix a problem is before you know it is a problem. The second-best time is as soon as you are aware of the problem and the third-best time is as soon as the fix is available to deploy. Very few organizations can solve within the best three options, thereby leaving *now* as the best time to solve the problem. *Now* is not a code word for your next change window. *Now* means the minute a release is available, because every hour, day, week, and month that goes by sees liability and risk for your organization increase.

In summary, DevOps practitioners have a fervor that has not been matched since Six Sigma or information privacy practitioners changed the world. Very few movements will have the passion you will come to expect from the culture of DevOps or DevSecOps.

In the next section, we will understand continual improvement.

DevOps Continuous

Eternal concepts are those that persist on a plane that is above and extremely hard for the human imagination to comprehend. To someone who is an expert in their discipline, the goal is to impact the world with their creation in an eternal way. While it is not possible to create something that lasts forever, perpetual concepts are still our aspirations. Indeed, perpetual motion is not achievable; however, the pursuit of a perpetual or evergreen solution is worthwhile.

On the path to trying to achieve an impossible goal, many breakthroughs are achieved that provide significant benefits for those positively affected both internally and externally. Society benefits from the solutions produced by each breakthrough. The breakthrough of the incandescent light bulb created the momentum necessary to provide electricity to most homes. Because electricity was installed in the home for the light bulb, additional use cases became possible. Today, many homes have only electric-powered systems throughout the home, as the danger of electrocution has been mitigated through hundreds of iterations.

CI/CD is the concept of continual integration and continual delivery or deployment of software releases. The concept is that software is always as imperfect as humanity itself, which causes all software releases to be less than perfect. The primary ROI for a software package is approximately 85% of perfection. This number is proven by purchase patterns in the market. Perfection is impossible, but through iteration, improvements continue to step the software closer to 100% perfection. Each iteration provides meaningful improvements in quality, performance, features, and security. Due to the pace of the market, threats, and human resources, a CI/CD model allows for the deployment of improvements in real time with the infinity cycle of DevOps practice.

Continuous everything is needed for success. Whatever noun you use to follow the word *continuous*, it would be a valid part of your strategy, practice, and culture.

In conclusion, improvement is the key to success with DevOps, and continual investment in culture and financial resources enables your organization to be prepared for problems that may cause a negative impact.

In the next section, we will understand when and how to act on information.

DevOps Act

Act, act, act – any action is better than no action when lives are at stake. In dangerous situations, the only consistent loser is the one who hesitates. Picture your worst reality, and any action taken in that reality will improve your odds of success. Reality treats those who act with a higher statistical probability of success. Most of our educational experience is focused on punishing action taken without thought, but in real life, action creates the opportunity for success.

See something, say something is a model that many law enforcement and marketing programs promote. If you see a problem, tell somebody so that action can be taken. This basic concept requires action and can save your organization from many types of failure. We want and need all developed software to notify of anything that could be a problem. Many security operations leverage software, which analyzes input from all available sources to automatically create a ticket if a pattern is determined that may be an issue to investigate. Additional analysis can be performed on reoccurring informational tickets or other patterns determined.

Act! If you are qualified to act when an issue or potential issue is noticed, act. We also want the software to take action as well.

Most organizations have automation capabilities such as an **Intrusion Prevention System** (**IPS**), but, have disabled that functionality due to fear of production impact or other unintentionally impacting action on the part of the software. We need that functionality tested on a regular basis and allowed to take action when a potential threat or adverse condition is noticed. A false action is an inconvenience, but failure to act as close to an event as possible can cost human life. Bankruptcy is a regular outcome of the failure to act when a problem first occurs, but this can escalate to prison if responsible parties fail to act further down the line.

To summarize, **ACT**!

In the next section, we will explain the DevOps impact on SASE.

DevOps Impact

The DevOps mindset is a doctrinal approach to continual improvement through secure development iterations. The two primary impacts on SASE from a DevOps perspective are security and reliability. Each iteration of the DevOps loop should produce a product that is more reliable and secure. Each iteration should cause material improvement over at least one aspect of the product or service. DevOps practice should cause us to think in a more perpetual fashion than our previous experiences would suggest.

The pressures in farming as an industry often cause overutilization of natural resources, which in turn destroys the resources necessary for successful farming. If DevOps methods were applied to farming, the natural resources available for farming would increase in both volume as well as quality. This continual improvement approach to farming would create increased productivity while reducing the consumption of natural resources.

In technology, the farming example is proven, as resource demands increase annually while productivity with existing resources declines. The reverse is also true, as the perceived low cost of resources has caused a sprawl effect that requires increased resources regularly to attempt sustenance. The reality is that the technology industry is failing. An example is the cost of data storage, which should decrease annually through efficiencies but is often a key threat to IT budgets, as data storage requirements increase annually through inefficiencies. Those inefficiencies offer little-to-no ROI for IT leaders to resolve. In a clean, efficient DevOps-based approach, the cancerous sprawl would be pruned routinely, which would result in lower annual costs related to data storage.

DevOps must be brutal in eliminating technical debts to provide an effective solution for secure communications systems.

Summary

SASE DevOps is simply an approach to solving the legacy issues in software development, by focusing on a successful operational model that continually improves throughout the production life cycle of each release of a specific SASE service.

The DevOps cultural approach to solving issues as they are made known is achieved through iterative releases of software that improve upon existing software in production. This improves time to market over previous models by up to 36 months and security by reducing up to 80% of computing system exposures.

DevSecOps is the long-term desired approach to all software development in the future.

In the next chapter, *SASE Forward*, we will start to understand forward thinking on SASE, understand how the present model is the baseline, understand the intentions for a future in SASE, create a measurement to apply to predictions, and explain the future of SASE as it stands.

19
SASE Forward

In the future, SASE services will be completely different from what is available today. Similar to the history of x86 computer hardware, it will be predictable and, therefore, a pattern emerges that allows the diligent to stay ahead of the next change.

The future is only predictable through the lens of history. Ignoring history has been the cause of the fall of many organizations, governments, countries, and whole civilizations that have ceased to exist. The further we can travel back in time through history, the more patterns become observable.

The future is very much a SASE services future. It is time to embrace the model of perpetual learning. It is time to realize that in the world, there are changes, threats, risks, issues, and barriers to success. The way to meet each new issue is through conquering your personal fears, your organizational fears, and your cultural fears.

A new model requires a perpetual state of change within your person, organization, and culture to survive. While this can often be overwhelming, the reality is that for every problem in life, there is a solution. Each solution requires action. Education and process will continue to lag behind the market, as both need a defined problem to solve. Your organization needs you and your team to outpace a written plan by noticing changes, finding solutions, and executing a new solution for which the plan is yet to be written.

Each week, we are faced with innovative technology and new terminology to describe how experts categorize it. **Secure Access Service Edge (SASE)** refers to a collective of security and secure communications services that will evolve daily in the near future. Each service included in the SASE category benefits from integration with another service. Each of the SASE services will evolve at its own pace, requiring CI/CD practices, DevSecOps, DevOps, and AIOps for ongoing success.

As far as we can see by looking at the market at the time of writing and into the future by 20 years, SASE will be the solution for secure communications. Will the name SASE survive? Only the future will tell, but the construction of the SASE model will survive for the next 20-plus years. The methods and approaches to SASE will survive, no matter what its name changes to. The model for understanding SASE in this book is simplistic by design to help you and your organization visualize a path forward in a sea of problems that are brought to you daily. This model will support your team for the next couple of decades, no matter what the experts call the iterations of the SASE concept.

In this chapter, we will discuss how to understand forward thinking on the SASE topic, understand how the present model is the baseline, understand the intentions for a future in SASE, create a measurement to apply to predictions, and explain the SASE future concept as we know it.

We will cover the following main topics in this chapter:

- Forward Overview – understand forward thinking in SASE
- Forward Present – understand how the present model is the baseline
- Forward Future – understand the intentions for a future in SASE
- Forward Measured – create a measurement to apply to predictions
- Forward Concept – explain the SASE future concept as we know it

Forward Overview

At the time of writing, there is no industry standard for SASE. We are currently expecting the standard to be published any day now. I have had the privilege of helping the brilliant minds that have been working to create standards for SASE with the MEF Forum for about 2 years. The people in that working group have collectively invested thousands of hours outside of their primary role to create an approach that will allow interoperability within competing SASE services. We appreciate industry analysts at Gartner, for noticing the pattern that we were each deploying into the market without collective knowledge of a trend. To each of us, it was a logical next step to solve problems that our customers presented, but the coining of the phrase SASE enabled us to create a focus on excellence in our individual SASE efforts.

To go forward, we must relearn our trade in the technology world. Getting into this industry, 30 years ago, we had to retrain every 3–5 years to be effective. Technology, at no point in history, has ever been a finite discipline. In fact, when studying all industries, you could make the same observation that no skill is ever truly mastered. An expert in a skill invests considerable time learning at the beginning of their career and hones that skill perpetually throughout their career to perpetually retain proficiency. Throughout their career, they are learning at what may appear to outsiders a less than 1% annual improvement pace. To the master of any skilled trade, they are learning daily, but the fine improvements in their craft are seldom newsworthy. With technology, millions of pages of news about changes are published daily, which creates the impression that progress is being made at light speed, but that is an oversold version of the truth.

Legitimate experts in any technology discipline do not refer to themselves as experts, as no such thing is possible. For example, when SD-WAN was first marketed, the product looked nothing like SD-WAN today and could not actually care for itself in production without significant care and feeding of the system. Within 3 years, there were close to 100 different SD-WAN products that all had different approaches to the concept of SD-WAN, even though many shared the same basic open-source code. Some companies had multiple SD-WAN products competing internally for investment and human capital. Recruiters scrambled for SD-WAN engineers and architects and used the term **Subject Matter Expert** (**SME**). The market may not have produced a hundred SME-type resources in the SD-WAN space over a 5-year period, but there were tens of thousands of jobs where recruiters expected SD-WAN experts. It took close to 5 years for the market to produce a certification program for SD-WAN. There were no experts to hire, which leads to the question of how honest the résumés were that led to a particular candidate receiving a job offer during that time period.

SME is a great marketing term for someone that does an excellent job designing, building, deploying, or operating a complex solution. SME is an effortless way to describe someone that has successfully leveraged a new solution in a way that brings value to their organization. The term is not the problem but, instead, the idea of proficiency is. Iterative improvement is the goal for each person in technology as well as in each aspect of the industry. It is much better that someone admits that they are not an expert and then apply themselves to becoming an expert. Rarely will the true expert realize when they cross the line from novice to SME. They will instead continue to improve on a path to an unattainable goal. The value, as with most things in life, is the pursuit of attainment, rather than achieving it. In life, the journey with the right attitude, perspective, work ethic, and discipline is worth much more than a lifetime achievement award.

In summary, expertise is not a defined achievement but the practice of iteration through practice in real-world application that provides consequences for failure and rewards for success.

In the next section, we will start to understand how the present model for SASE is the baseline for the future.

Forward Present

The present model for SASE is the baseline for the future. In conversation, the practical application of the *Zero Trust Framework* has been an impossible goal. In fact, with every challenging goal throughout history, the next achievement is always considered impossible to those rational thinkers that talk through the reasons why achievement will be forever elusive. It is good to be rational, but it may be impossible to find a financial benefit to rational thinking.

While great minds consider a problem rationally, there is often someone in the next room that is executing a solution to the problem by leveraging less than rational methods, such as trial and error.

SASE services are production-ready and have been so prior to the writing of this book. Many thousands of organizations have been operating SASE in production, with a few hundred having a **Zero Trust Framework** (**ZTF**) in place. It is worth noting that many conversations taking place at the time this book was written are about how we can implement an academically perfect version of SASE or a ZTF. The reality is that we cannot implement a perfect solution; we can, however, implement a working solution that is incrementally improved through iterative methodology, as we have discussed throughout the book. It is not perceived financially feasible to create a perfect ZTF-based solution, as it would ensure that no device, system, or human would ever have access to it. By definition, all devices, systems, and humans accessing any resource are a threat to security and are not to be trusted. For a positive **User Experience** (**UX**), access to organizational resources is required, and therefore, we must live with an imperfect security environment that is continually improved through our cultural approach to security.

The right framework to move forward with is a ZTF, which is and should be the baseline for all SASE services. A ZTF is a framework, approach, model, method, practice, and system for achieving effective security with a positive UX. ZTF and UX are mentioned here to apply focus to each word and what it really means to an organization. A ZTF allows the integration of all applications, systems, identification mechanisms, security policies, operations platforms, and anything else necessary to operate via an API. The more resources are integrated into a ZTF, the better it performs. A ZTF is not a product but a security framework approach to ensuring optimal security for your organization. A ZTF needs to be applied to all types of security, including physical security for your organization's physical environments and assets such as buildings, automobiles, tools, video, paper documents, office supplies, and anything else the organization controls.

In summary, a ZTF is the framework for the future and is presently in production in many organizations.

In the next section, we will start to understand the intentions for a future in SASE.

Forward Future

The future will see an explosion in the market of the number of services that become part of the SASE ecosystem. At the time of writing, dozens of services have been classified as SASE across many different service providers, software developers, and system integrators. SASE should be considered synonymous with any security product or service and most network services going forward. The key to effective SASE remains integration to allow each service to communicate and mitigate issues created across an ecosystem.

An API backbone solution is a key component to reducing the amount of effort and time required to integrate each new service as soon as it is subscribed to by any part of an organization. Integration that takes longer than 1 day will become unacceptable to any organization, and real-time integration within seconds of subscription will become the new normal pace of integration.

Artificial Intelligence for IT Operations (**AIOps**), which may have been considered a luxury, will be a requirement for all future technology solutions, as the massive volume of system and service notifications cannot be sorted through or acted upon by human labor. The problem, in turn, requires action by a system in real time when an issue occurs. Action is necessary prior to the compounding of any issues into a problem.

Increasing security regulation will both require automation and insurance against a liability created by automated attacks. In turn, a compliance practice must implement active compliance testing, as monthly, quarterly, and annual audits will be considered negligent behavior. The compliance systems should be actively interrogating all organizational resources to ensure 100% compliance at all times. This process ensures that all misconfigurations are found, reported, corrected, and documented within seconds.

In conclusion, the path going forward requires all IT functions to be automated for an organization to avoid financial, legal, and regulatory consequences.

In the next section, we will create a measurement to apply to predictions.

Forward Measured

How do you measure the future? How do you predict what is going to happen and when? A correct response is that you cannot measure the future; however, without measurement, how do you prepare?

In actuality, the future is predictable, as every living thing follows a pattern of behavior that has minor variances. If we simply study the history of a subject that we would like to predict future outcomes for, we can see a pattern in reverse, starting from today and going back to inception. To predict the future outcome, we place the timeline from today going forward, leveraging the ratios and frequencies from the historical pattern, and applying the same pattern to the future. The frequency of repetition or iteration when studied from inception to the present shows slower, faster, or stable occurrences of the pattern, which we can apply to our future prediction with the assumption that the pattern will be repeated until catastrophic circumstances cause it to change. Without catastrophe, most patterns will remain true.

Prediction is a combination of art and science that, when studied actively and corrected as needed, can produce reasonably accurate predictions. Financial forensics can produce solid predictions on which an entire economy can be planned. Failure of equipment can be predicted, allowing just-in-time maintenance that is scheduled hours before a necessary part is due to fail. The more data that is available, and the longer the data sampling period, the more accurate the prediction becomes.

With SASE, the future can be measured in terms of the life cycle of a software release. If we take one particular SASE service and analyze the software that service replaced, such as SD-WAN replacing routing, we are able to create a statistical understanding of the evolution timeline from a legacy perspective. We must then study the variance in behavior with the timeline information available on the current generation of software. This indicates a change in the frequency of release that must then be applied to the pattern.

For a particular router software, studying the evolutionary timeline of software releases since the 1.0 version of that router provides a baseline. The SD-WAN equivalent from the same manufacturer will be a completely different code that dirties the data from an analysis perspective. Both software release timelines must be studied for the legacy and current solutions to understand the difference in frequencies between versions `1.0`, `2.0`, `3.0`, and `1.1`, `1.2`, and `1.3` as a model. The prediction requires a little art in that the baseline of the legacy and the current software must be overlaid to understand acceleration, but the two timelines in parallel provide outer boundaries to create a range of release frequency.

For our example vendor, who will remain nameless, they had major releases at approximately 34 months and minor releases at approximately 8 months on their legacy router. They had major releases at approximately 7 months and minor releases at approximately 1.5 months on their minor releases. This created a 7–34-month major and 1.5–8-month minor range. History shows that this company has a pattern of normalizing new software to its legacy pattern of release after approximately 36 months from its initial acquisition or development. The oscillation from new to stable within the development ecosystem causes us to look at an adjusted release of new software somewhere in the 30–40% range, as normalized by the company. This information causes us to predict future releases as falling in the 9–12-month range for major and around 59 days for minor releases.

Please note that these predictions are not expected to be perfect math, as human behavior is involved. If, in the future, machines are performing an AI-based DevSecOps function, whereby they are developing the code we are using, the prediction models will actually become a more sanitary math problem. Other pollutants to a sanitary model for prediction are external factors, such as political, environmental, economic, and other newsworthy contributors to variance.

Leveraging this prediction model, we can determine that a generational life cycle of the software our SASE service depends on evolves into something significantly different every 9–12 months. This requires retraining of the entire staff every 9–12 months to ensure successful operations of the new SASE service.

In general, the market is evolving to the point where every 6–18 weeks, at least one major release of the software will evolve by 70–90%, requiring support personnel to learn new features, functions, and, in some cases, a new methodology for support.

To summarize, the technology evolutionary cycle that feels out of control is predictable. Since it is predictable, you can prepare your organization for the next evolution.

In the next section, we will explain the SASE future concept as we know it.

Forward Concept

Going forward, the concept for SASE is to secure all communications from any device, system, application, or user to any other device, system application, or user by leveraging active, automated, autonomous, and aggressive security solutions.

SASE is expected to be the secure-communications replacement for legacy routers, firewalls, and VPN solutions. It accounts for all available input mechanisms for analysis. SASE is based on an ZTF, which requires a change in thought process for all technology professionals everywhere.

A forward concept is an idea in which we leverage fully integrated services to achieve policy-based goals for our organizations. This can be accomplished by leveraging many systems that are in production today. However, any system that cannot accommodate a ZTF must be eliminated from a production environment quickly.

The market has asked for consideration of parallel environments or hybrid ZTF and legacy security models. There is no benefit to a ZTF if lesser security framework models are left in place. The market will leave legacy solutions in production decades beyond their commitments to retire those systems, as their decision to do so is based on the cost of replacement. The cost of retention of legacy systems can be extremely difficult to measure and compare to the cost of new offerings. Parallel security models consistently land their organization in the news for the security failures of retaining systems that have poor security. The cost of legal, financial, and physical security breaches is often catastrophic to an organization that tried to save money on security.

The future has compute power everywhere. Compute is not a data center or cloud concept; it is, however, a pervasive concept in the future. Latency-centered application design requires consistent 3-milliseconds-or-less response times to compute. Blockchain technology will allow us to use generic compute from any source for distributed ledger-type functions. All fixed devices will become part of a shared chain with the ability to monetize any compute available anywhere. Imagine that every compute system in the world allowed anyone in proximity to securely access system resources for a nano-sized application to run for a transaction that takes seconds. After the transaction is completed, the chain is returned to the cloud, and any local software is removed and scrubbed from the system.

In the future, while walking down the street, an application is functioning on your smartwatch that is interacting with dozens of computers that are owned by anyone across a 6G cellular network. Each computer owner is paid for their system processing time through a distributed ledger system that they subscribed to. Each session established by your watch is secured by a ZTF with a SASE service that you subscribe to. Every trace of your activity is securely scrubbed from each system, with your chain being updated to your private cloud instance. All of the technology required for this solution is available today.

Summary

SASE Forward, everything will change for the better. The key problem to solve is how quickly humans can adapt to this solution. For effective secure communications services to function, operations, development, and support organizations must merge into one fluid team that is materially learning at least one new skill every 2 weeks. To prioritize education is to allocate increasing amounts of the work week to education. It is possible that most agile teams are those whose leadership places 20–25% of their workweek into new educational models that incentivize performance and the demonstration of new skills required by the organization.

The future is predictable based on an analysis of the past. The future is SASE at the pace we can consume it.

In the next chapter, *SASE Bonus*, we will start to understand SD-WAN from a basic perspective, understand the SD-WAN design best practices, feel the failure of thousands of poor designs, experience the success of correct designs, and explain the best practices for SD-WAN design, which are all part of your SASE journey.

20
SASE Bonus

The first several years of SD-WAN solutions consistently failed in production. This failure was primarily due to an overall lack of understanding of the differences between legacy, routed WAN solutions and the new SD-WAN solutions that leveraged policy differently to forward traffic instead of relying on the routing protocols. The disaggregation of data and control plan for policy-based decision-making in SD-WAN effectively grandfathered much of the skill of the world's best network engineers. SD-WAN felt as if programmers purposely sought to eliminate network engineering as a skill in favor of active software-based decision-making.

It is interesting that the WAN engineer and the SD-WAN engineer can have an entire conversation using the same words but with two distinctly separate definitions for each word. Both WAN and SD-WAN designs use routing and policy but in completely different ways from each other. In fact, it has often been easier to teach SD-WAN to someone unskilled in routing than a seasoned network engineer due to the same concepts being utilized differently in each context.

Designing SD-WAN solutions is much more complex than a routed WAN with an identical scale. Integration of multiple circuits across routers can be established by configuring a dynamic routing protocol that leverages all available routes. In contrast, each SD-WAN path must be considered independently, and policies designed to give the orchestrator as much autonomy as possible in selecting the ideal path for each packet or flow.

Even though SD-WAN design is more complex, it does not build on legacy skills. SD-WAN requires humility to learn a new way of designing and operating a network. It can be extremely hard for talented humans to start over again with new rules for success. SD-WAN offers the possibility of self-healing within the design; however, the old rules applied to the new technology prohibit this level of success.

SD-WAN, as with any evolutionary technology, has the ability to cause as much damage as it does to create new value. Each of us must take the time to understand what success looks like and how to achieve it with each new generation of technology.

In this chapter, we will come to understand SD-WAN from a basic perspective, understand SD-WAN design best practices, feel the failure of thousands of poor designs, experience the success of correct designs, and learn how to explain best practices for SD-WAN design.

We will cover the following main topics in this chapter:

- SD-WAN Overview – understand SD-WAN from a basic perspective
- SD-WAN Design – understand SD-WAN design best practice
- SD-WAN Failure – feel the failure from thousands of poor designs
- SD-WAN Experience – experience the success of correct designs
- SD-WAN Practice – explain best practices for the SD-WAN design

SD-WAN Overview

Before we delve deeper, it is important to know what SD-WAN is. **SD-WAN** stands for **Software-Defined Wide Area Network**. As the name suggests, SD-WAN utilizes a software mechanism as defined in the policy to make path selection decisions as opposed to routing protocols. SD-WAN consists of hardware devices and software implemented across a highly distributed system. It uses software instead of routers to direct digital traffic.

SD-WAN can leverage any physical type of connection to forward traffic across. Commonly, SD-WAN will use private network connections such as MPLS, Metro Ethernet, dedicated fiber Ethernet, point-to-point wireless, or private satellite and cellular connections. Public connectivity to the internet across 4G, 5G, broadband, or satellite connections is used on an equal basis as all connections are securely tunneled with equal levels of encryption and treated as insecure. In this way, both public and private network paths are treated as VPNs and all data is tunneled end-to-end for secure communications.

With SD-WAN, you can manage the entire network with one central user interface. This form of management is commonly called an orchestrator. Instead of configuring SD-WAN physical, virtual, or cloud-based devices on an individual basis, all devices may be configured simultaneously from the orchestrator. The orchestrator leverages templates that may be pushed, audited, enforced, and updated in real time across all devices at once.

SD-WAN provides software-based decision mechanisms that score performance across all available data paths actively. These scores are considered in conjunction with SD-WAN policies to determine the available path to securely forward data.

SD-WAN solution components are as follows:

- **Edges**: Easy-to-install appliances for your remote branches that come in physical, virtual, or cloud-native instances.
- **Gateways**: Optimized access to cloud applications and data centers at top-tier network points of presence. Gateways are not leveraged with all vendors but often an edge device may be deployed in a gateway role to provide the same function as that of a gateway between environments.

- **Controllers**: Provide centralized control of the data flow through the cloud network and can make dynamic per-packet or per-flow changes based on performance or policy.
- **Orchestrators**: Provide centralized, enterprise-wide installation, configuration, and real-time monitoring.

The market embraced SD-WAN quickly due to perceived cost savings forecasted by industry analysts at up to 90% cost savings over MPLS-based WAN solutions. The cost savings are real, however, the lack of skill in the market caused most organizations significant project cost overruns with reduced network availability. The reality was that the rapid transition from circuits with 99.999% availability to circuits with 85-92% availability that were also on the internet created downtime for many services across many organizations. Over several years, the solution was determined to be a right-sized mix of MPLS and broadband that increased bandwidth, reduced latency, and balanced cost savings with reliability.

In summary, SD-WAN offers significant value over legacy WAN solutions but excessive market hype costs organizations dearly while the technology matures.

In the next section, we will establish an understanding of SD-WAN design best practices.

SD-WAN Design

SD-WAN benefits from the DevOps mindset. With DevOps, the steps in the process flow are basically: *Plan, Code, Build, Test, Release, Continuous Deployment and Continuous Integration, Operate, Monitor through Continuous Feedback Loop, Notify,* and *Action*. With a legacy WAN solution, the planning stage was the primary focus, and it was thought that design perfection will be achieved. With SD-WAN, perfection is only achieved through dynamic iteration. This can also be considered the CI/CD-based optimization process. SD-WAN design works better with an implementation of a **Proof of Concept (POC)**, then pilot, then full production implementations. Each implementation is then optimized through the DevOps process, even if no code is modified but the solution is refined through the process.

The best SD-WAN design starts with a high-level design that takes into consideration the requirements, such as sites, circuits, bandwidth per site, aggregate hub bandwidth requirements, cloud services providers in production, and all applications in production. While this may feel excessive, all of this information is required to develop an effective solution. The key concept at this point is that while WAN solutions are designed based on layers 1-3 of the OSI model, SD-WAN solutions are designed across layers 1-7, with special consideration to the end-user experience.

The next differentiation between WAN and SD-WAN design is that the POC is a key requirement for finding all unknown applications. Across more than 4,000 organizations, we found that not a single organization was fully aware of all applications in production within their organization. Unfortunately, many organizations only became aware of applications after they established policies that negatively affected the performance of the unknown applications to the point where business operations were affected. The POC, when executed correctly, acts as the key discovery component of the environment that allows the project team to finalize the planning stage. When implementing the POC within production sites, which is required for success, it is important to install the SD-WAN appliances in parallel to the existing WAN devices so they can be swapped between production and test roles as needed for emergencies. After the POC phases are complete, the POC sites may become a part of the production pilot.

A sampling size of 5-10% of the sites is sufficient for the production pilot. The pilot phase requires a mixture of the different site types such as large, medium, and small, remote workers, data centers, and CSP. Site typing is necessary to scale as many of the SD-WAN concepts are variable and consequently require more flexibility than bandwidth-centric design. Custom designs per site are discouraged as it restricts the SD-WAN performance flexibility. Generally, 3-5 site types are all that are required for success, and organizations with many site types have less success in production than organizations with fewer site types.

SD-WAN design is successful when all legacy routing policies such as **Policy-Based Routing** (PBR) and **Quality of Service** (QoS) or **Class of Service** (CoS) mechanisms are removed. SD-WAN leverages software-defined quality mechanisms that are dynamic in nature. Legacy QOS and COS mechanisms effectively prevent SD-WAN's benefits by force, fixing configuration that may have been perfect on the day it was configured but is not flexible when circumstances change. When applying SD-WAN to a legacy configured circuit, all SD-WAN traffic may be forwarded across a single COS instead of all available bandwidth. You must design SD-WAN correctly and then trust the software to perform. Trust and verify that both performance and security standards are being achieved with the solution.

SD-WAN edge device templates can be set up with all the basic configuration details, whereby a new appliance may be shipped directly from the manufacturer to a site without customization. The device, when arriving at the site, may be connected to the internet, pointed to its orchestrator, and then activated. Upon activation, it is upgraded to match the production software, receives the base template, establishes secure tunnels, and achieves production status within a matter of a few minutes.

Policy templates should be simple and serve as small a function as possible. By keeping each policy to the **Minimum Viable Product** (MVP), the policy may be stacked hierarchically and then compounded as needed. Keeping each policy to the MVP allows for automation mechanisms for orchestrators, AIOps, and active security solutions to adjust policy as needed within milliseconds. This is the concept of least prescriptive or least restrictive. Allowing automation of compound policies often creates unintended consequences. Creating a library of MVP-based policies allows for greater automation over time.

Routing must be redesigned for effective SD-WAN solutions. Often, we create something that looks like a network of stub routes instead of a well-designed routed network. Most SD-WAN solutions do not need complex routing such as was required with legacy WAN solutions. The SD-WAN solution will leverage the routing table to understand the environment but will attempt to forward traffic based on the best quality score for a particular path as opposed to the rules of a specific routing protocol.

In summary, the key concepts are to deploy POC, deploy pilot, leverage site typing, establish hierarchical templating, create least prescriptive policies, simplify routing, remove QoS, and trust the software-based decision making.

In the next section, we will feel the failure of thousands of poor designs.

SD-WAN Failure

Failure is a hard teacher. Often, pride restricts learning from failures. The baby that learns to walk learns from trial and error. From each minor failure causing the baby to fall, the baby learns what does not work and emerges from failure as a successful toddler. The toddler is not perfect at the skill of walking but continues to learn from failure. The child not only walks without falling but also runs with the skills learned through failures. Emotionally, failure feels like a permanent, defining record that cannot be overcome. Objective intellectual analysis of failure is a key resource for learning if we can move past the emotional impact.

Every organization has a stress experience caused by cost pressures. When talking to thousands of companies each year about technology requirements, every organization at some point explains that they, unlike other organizations, are unable to afford the latest solution due to unique cost pressures. In reality, we are all faced with the same issue: we do not have unlimited funds to pursue perfection in any area of our life or work. Unfortunately, since many leaders believe that their situation is unique and requires a creative solution to help their organization if the market declares a cost-saving strategy, it must be considered immediately. In reality, when studying thousands of projects, the successful projects were those that had the least customization. The fact is that while organizations are unique in many aspects of their business, their actual needs are fairly similar when it comes to technology projects. More than 80% of customization expenditure is wasted and, in turn, cause the ongoing operational costs to deliver a negative ROI.

With SD-WAN, the market ran to achieve the savings that were talked about in every article. The solution was to eliminate expensive MPLS circuits and leverage inexpensive internet connectivity from any source. Ultimately, the SD-WAN movement was a great way to save money that was considered factual as everyone in the market agreed at least in perception.

The market tried to achieve cost savings through SD-WAN at any cost. Unfortunately, the market had no skilled SD-WAN **Subject Matter Expert (SME)** to rely on. Technical education for SD-WAN has lagged behind the market for several years. Each manufacturer had less than 100 SME resources at a product launch for millions of customers asking for their share of cost savings. The manufacturer training was often a simple overview and configuration guide that created more questions than answers.

The results from the first three years in the SD-WAN market had tens of thousands of organizations trying to start an SD-WAN project but less than 3% actually got more than 10 total sites per organization installed. By year five, less than 10% actually completed their SD-WAN project. For each that completed a full SD-WAN project, the one-time costs averaged 300% of the initial estimates, took three to five times as long to implement as forecasted, and required repurchase and installation of private circuits that had been displaced.

Technical failures in the first three years of global SD-WAN implementations caused issues such as applications orphaned, sites orphaned, full network outages, voice outages, artificial bandwidth throttling, site outages lasting more than a week, project cancellation, and complete reversal of the project that removed SD-WAN for more than a year.

From a hardware perspective, many organizations had to upgrade hardware purchased more than once per site due to physical performance limitations of hardware due to excessive processing overhead from the software as designed by the manufacturer. In many cases, this was due to concurrent tunneling requirements for mesh and partial mesh designs.

In conclusion, failure is a great teacher, and SD-WAN failures are typical anytime a known technology undergoes an evolutionary change. The primary failures of SD-WAN could have been solved by a greater focus on education. The market pressure for cost savings drove greater acceptance of the market hype, which in turn, forced technology teams to try and leverage the new technology prior to maturity.

In the next section, we will experience the success of correct designs.

SD-WAN Experience

Based on the broad market failure of SD-WAN projects, service providers that studied their failure and adapted their strategy based on that hard education have been able to help clients achieve SD-WAN success. The organizations that have successfully installed SD-WAN across all or the majority of their sites have leveraged many of the lessons learned from the failed projects.

Today, there are production SD-WAN networks that consist of more than 10,000 sites. These implementations are generally a hub-and-spoke or dual hub-and-spoke design. Over time, the mechanisms required for successful full mesh designs will be refined allowing full mesh with minimal overhead. The early days of SD-WAN required three to five times the hardware cost to support the active management of large quantities of tunnels. Compare this with the fact that the average router installed over the history of routing managed one connection that had no encryption. The processor overhead for tunnel management with encryption and other security requirements has made full mesh designs for SD-WAN cost prohibitive.

Successful large-scale SD-WAN implementations have kept configuration at a minimum with light policies that are least prescriptive. These implementations rely on the manufacturer's SD-WAN software to make the majority of traffic forwarding decisions. Traffic only drops to the underlay circuit as a rare exception when all other paths are ruled out. One of the early failures was to treat the underlay as a normal path for traffic if the circuit was a private connection. By designing for all traffic to utilize the overlay path and making the underlay the last resort path, the policy design issues are worked out, which leaves a dynamic, self-healing solution in production.

One of the repetitive patterns with successful SD-WAN projects was that the WAN routing protocol was standardized to a single protocol. In almost every case studied, **Border Gateway Protocol (BGP)** was the winner, with all other protocols being isolated to LAN. This decision was primarily due to open-source software contributions that most SD-WAN manufacturers are leveraging in their code. In addition to the market commonality for BGP in SDN use cases, it appears that the market was waiting for a reason to standardize, and the SD-WAN project became that reason to commit to BGP.

Route or path visibility for SD-WAN generally extends one hop into the LAN, which was not required with legacy WAN routing. The SD-WAN software needs to be aware of applications and networks available as resources to forward traffic. To enable this visibility if the LAN leverages another protocol, that protocol is redistributed into BGP for the benefit of the SD-WAN solution's visibility.

SD-WAN benefits generally start with two or more circuits in production. WAN routing often leveraged a primary circuit and a backup circuit. With SD-WAN, the new expectation is that all available circuits are leveraged in parallel for traffic forwarding that is determined by policy but can provide the aggregate benefit of all available bandwidth similar to load balancing. One successful strategy executed across these projects has been to leverage both MPLS and broadband or MPLS and 4G/5G on the same device. When hardware redundancy is required, the two circuits are either split between devices, duplicated on multiple devices, or abstracted with dual homed switching external to the SD-WAN appliance. Many organizations achieved SD-WAN installation across thousands of sites in less than six months by installing a 4G/5G cellular data connection as the only circuit for each site and later received a second wireline circuit at a later stage in the project. The SD-WAN policy makes the transition between circuits seamless for the end user without a production outage.

To summarize, by learning a new approach to implementing the new technology, many organizations were able to successfully complete their SD-WAN projects.

In the next section, we will explain best practices for SD-WAN design.

SD-WAN Practice

The best practice for SD-WAN design requires new logic leveraged for what seems to be an old task. With legacy WAN projects, the greatest network engineers and architects spent months planning every detail, which resulted in a forced compliance model for success. PBR enforced behaviors for traffic across the network to attempt to guarantee performance. With SD-WAN, any forced behavior will lead to failure, as the software continually evolves every few weeks. Network conditions are always changing, which caused the legacy design to consider every lesson learned to that point. The point of software-defined networking is that all possible conditions cannot be known, therefore, the software has to be dynamic and somewhat autonomous in the way it self-heals and self-tunes.

Best practice rules for success are as follows:

- **First rule**: Keep the design as simple as possible. The SD-WAN edge device gets an MVP configuration that basically connects it to the network and connects to the orchestrator. Each policy must be an MVP. Each policy can be stacked hierarchically but should not be a compound policy in itself.
- **Second rule**: Remove all legacy design components and simplify routing. Strip out the CoS/QoS mechanisms, standardize on one routing protocol, remove traffic shaping, remove PBR if possible, leverage dynamic IP addressing, and allow the SD-WAN software to make as many decisions as possible.

- **Third rule**: Create site types and templates for each site type. Present the stakeholders with a range of three to five site types and not more than seven site types. Each additional site type creates overhead and reduces automation efficiencies. Each site type gets a template built in the orchestrator as an MVP. Each site is assigned to a site type that may change over time as the needs of that site change.
- **Final rule**: Learn from failure. Design, build, deploy, optimize, and repeat….

Summary

SD-WAN has reached maturity, and each SD-WAN product in the market is going through a generational life cycle of its software every 6 to 18 weeks. On the surface, that statement is incongruent. Unfortunately, it is true that SD-WAN is now mature and is also constantly evolving. The best practice for both SD-WAN and SASE will be to follow the DevOps mindset in a constant improvement or iterative fashion. There is no perfect design but the pursuit of perfection through iteration, improvement, and optimization, continually, is the most valuable best practice in the market at this time.

The goal is to create or implement something that provides immediate value to the organization and then immediately improve upon its value. When CI/CD practices are culturally embedded in your organization, the optimal value is achieved.

SASE Conclusion

Thank you for taking the time to read this book. My hope is that you will leverage this content to improve the way employees grow in your organization. Each wave of new technology increases the need to reinvent ourselves to both take advantage of the benefits of the improvements and also to help our organization to reinvent itself. Each organization has to add value to the lives of those it serves, or the organization will disappear at the point where its value diminishes beyond a sustainable level. As humans, we desire a legacy that lives past our mortality. The value of that legacy is determined by the value it provided to the world and, ultimately, the humans that benefited from that value. If you have questions after reading this book, please feel free to look me up on LinkedIn and connect with me there. You may also reach out to Packt's customer service staff and request that a follow-up book be written about any chapter here that would provide an informational deep dive into the content of that chapter. I am also available for public speaking engagements or seminars on the topics contained within the book.

The value of this book is determined by how you use the information that I have provided. My sincere desire is that I add some value to your life and the lives that are touched by what you do with this information.

Appendix
SASE Terms

The following acronyms are documented for convenience as they relate to the content in this book. It is recommended that you review the following terms and review the content related to any unfamiliar terms. In addition to reviewing the content, each unfamiliar term should be researched on the internet for more information. Excellent definitions may be found within the *NIST*, *MEF*, and *IEEE* websites:

- `https://www.nist.gov/`
- `https://www.mef.net/`
- `https://www.ieee.org/`

Acronym	Term
AAC	Actor Access Connection
ADS	Application Delivery Services
AFS	Application Flow Specifications
AIOps	Artificial Intelligence for IT Operations or Artificial Intelligence Operations Platform
Anti-X	Antimalware/Antivirus
API	Application Programming Interface
AR	Augmented Reality
BGP	Border Gateway Protocol
BI	Browser Isolation
CAPEX	Capital Expense
CASB	Cloud Access Security Broker

Acronym	Term
CDN	Content Delivery Network
CE	Customer Edge
CI/CD	Continuous Integration/Continual Development or Deployment
CoE	Center of Excellence
CoS	Class of Service
COTS	Common or Commercial off the Shelf
CSP	Cloud Service Provider
DevOps	Software Development combined with IT Operations
DevSecOps	Software Development combined with Security and IT Operations
DLP	Data Loss Prevention
DM	Device Management
DNF	Domain Name Filtering
DNS	Domain Name System
DPF	DNS Protocol Filtering
DPS	Device Posture Support
DSL	Domain Specific Language
EDR	Endpoint Detection and Response
EP	Endpoint Protection
EPC	Endpoint Connectivity
ERP	Enterprise Resource Planning
ES	Endpoint Security

Acronym	Term
FWaaS	Firewall as a Service
IAM or IdAM	Identity and Access Management
IDPS	Intrusion Detection and Prevention System (IDS/IPS)
IDS	Intrusion Detection System
IoT	Internet of Things
IP-P	IP Proxy
IPPF	IP, Port, and Protocol Filtering
IPS	Intrusion Prevention System
KPI	Key Performance Indicator
LAN	Local Area Network
MAC	Media Access Control
MBF	Middle Box Function
MCSE	Microsoft Certified Systems Engineer
MD+R	Malware Detection and Removal
MDM	Mobile Device Management
MDSO	Multi-Domain Service Orchestrator
MEF	The Metro Ethernet Forum or The MEF Forum
MFA	Multi-Factor Authentication
MSP	Managed Service Provider

Acronym	Term
MVP	Minimum Viable Product
NGFW	Next-Generation Firewall
NIST	National Institute of Standards and Technology
NMS	Network Management System
OPEX	Operational Expense
OSI	Open Systems Interconnection
OSS	Operations Support Systems
OT	Operational Technology
PE	Provider Edge
PEP	Policy End Point
PIN	Personal Identification Number
PVC	Permanent Virtual Circuit
QoS	Quality of Service
RBI	Remote Browser Isolation
ROI	Return on Investment
ROSI	Return on Security Investment
SaaS	Software as a Service
SASE	Secure Access Service Edge
SD	Software-Defined
SDNS	Secure Domain Name System
SDNSP	Secure Domain Name System Proxy

Acronym	Term
SD-WAN	Software-Defined Wide Area Network
SIEM	Security Information and Event Management
SLA	Service Level Agreement
SME	Subject Matter Expert
SOC	Secure or Security Operations Center
SSE	Security Service Edge
SSL	Secure Sockets Layer
SWG	Secure Web Gateway
TI	Threat Intelligence
TLS	Transport Layer Security
UBEA	User and Entity Behavior Analytic/User and Event Behavior Analytics
UNI	User Network Interface
URLF	Uniform Resource Locator Filtering
UTM	Unified Threat Management
UX	End User Experience or User Experience
WAF	Web Application Firewall
WAN	Wide Area Network
WAN-X	Wide Area Network Acceleration and Optimization
ZT	Zero Trust
ZTF	Zero Trust Framework
ZTNA	Zero Trust Network Access

Index

A

access identity 63-65
actor 53, 54
Actor Access Connection (AAC) 45
Agile 12
Agile Manifesto
   reference link 12
AI Operations Platform (AIOps) 25, 31
API manager 24, 87
Application Flow Specification (AFS) 55, 75
Application Programming Interface (API) 9, 24, 29, 87
Artificial Intelligence (AI) 13, 48, 88
Artificial Intelligence for IT Operations (AIOps) 9, 36, 86, 87, 144
Augmented Reality (AR) 16
Automation
   of management functions 90

B

Border Gateway Protocol (BGP) 154
Browser Isolation (BI) 74
business stakeholders 96, 97
business value 97

C

Capital Expense (CAPEX) 5
Centers of Excellence (COE) 22
Cisco Certified Network Professional (CCNP) 32
Class of Service (CoS) 152
Cloud Access Security Broker (CASB) 4, 72
cloud cost management 25, 87
Cloud Service Providers (CSPs) 20, 28, 37, 103
co-management 20, 21
Common Off-The-Shelf (COTS) 37
context identity 66
Continuous Integration/ Continual Delivery (CI/CD) 12, 133, 135
Customer Edge (CE) 53

D

Data Leakage Prevention (DLP) 74
Data Loss Prevention (DLP) 45
Development-Operations (DevOps) 5
   act on information 138
   continual improvement 137
   fervor 136, 137

impact 139
   overview 134, 135
Digital Identity Guidelines, Implementation Resources
   reference link 64
dimensional identity 65
DNS Protocol Filtering (DPF) 73
Domain Name Filtering (DNF) 74

E

effective management 21
effective policy 61
Endpoint Connectivity (EPC) 45
Enterprise Resource Planning (ERP) 109

F

Fifth-Generation Cellular (5G) 10
Firewall-as-a-Service (FWaaS) 78, 104

G

Gartner Hype Cycle 7
   reference link 7
Go-To-Market (GTM) practices 5

H

hack 126
hackers 126
Hack License 126
how statement 106
human behavior 14, 15
human issue 11, 12
human patterns 16, 17
human problem 13, 14
human solution 15, 16

I

Identity and Access Management Function (IdAM or IAM) 61
Identity and Access Management (IAM) 45, 53, 64
IEEE
   URL 157
Information Technology Infrastructure Library (ITIL) 134
integrate identity 67, 68
Intellectual Property (IP) 133
Internet of Things (IoT) 81
Intrusion Detection System (IDS) 4, 75
Intrusion Prevention System (IPS) 4, 66, 72, 74, 138
IP, Port, and Protocol Filtering (IPPF) 74
IP Proxy (IP-P) 74
iteration 12

J

Just-in-Time (JIT) 113, 131

K

Key Performance Indicators (KPIs) 97

L

learning model 127-130
   leverage, timing 131
   need, explaining 131
   overview 126, 127
learning model, modality 130
   ability 130
   deduction 130
   expectation 130

habit 130
inability 130
obligation 130
permission 130
possibility 130
least privilege security 67

M

Machine Learning (ML) 32
Malware Detection and Removal (MD+R) 74
managed SASE 21-23
Managed Services Provider (MSP) 4, 20, 39
management functions
   automation 90
management systems 88, 89
management templates 89
master orchestration platform 24, 87, 88
Mean Opinion Score (MOS) 59
Media Access Control (MAC) address 53
MEF 95 Policy-Driven Orchestration standard 59
MEF Forum's SASE Services Definition (MEF W117) 74
Metro Ethernet Forum (MEF) 4
   URL 157
Microsoft Active Directory (AD) 45
Microsoft Certified Systems Engineer (MCSE) 32
Middle Box Function (MBF) 74
Minimum Viable Product (MVP) 102, 114, 135, 152
modality 130
Multi-Domain Service Orchestrator (MDSO) 24, 31, 87
Multi-Factor Authentication (MFA) 48, 53, 76, 117
Multiprotocol Label Switching (MPLS) 7

N

National Institute of Standards and Technology (NIST) 64
   URL 64, 157
Network Management System (NMS) 24, 31, 87
New-to-Market (NTM) technology 7
Next-Generation Firewall (NGFW) 4, 118

O

Open Systems Interconnection (OSI) model 44, 118, 121
Operating Expense (OPEX) 5
operational SASE 23
Operational Technology (OT) 98
Operations Support Systems (OSSs) 68
orchestrated modes
   benefits 31
orchestration 7
Original Equipment Manufacturer (OEM) 4
overlapping policy 59

P

Permanent Virtual Connection (PVC) 53
Personal Identification Number (PIN) 65
policy 57
Policy-Based Routing (PBR) 152
Policy Endpoint (PEP) 45
Possibility 130
Project Management Institute-Project Management Professional (PMI-PMP) 9
project plan 129

Proof of Concept (POC) 129, 130, 151
Proof of Value (POV) 129, 130
Provider Edge (PE) 53

Q

Quality of Service (QoS) 59, 152

R

Return on Investment (ROI) 5, 37, 96, 109, 134
Return on Security Investment (ROSI) 6

S

SASE Actor Access Connection Policies 58, 60
SASE Composite Policy 58
SASE Context Policy 58
SASE design
  communication 114
  function 112
  operational support 113
  overview 110, 111
  theory 112
SASE DevOps
  action 135
  build 135
  CI/CD 135
  code 135
  monitor 135
  notify 135
  operate 135
  plan 135
  release 135
  start over at 1 with iteration 135
  test 135

SASE dynamic policies 60
SASE Edge 52
SASE effective policies 61
SASE Identity Policy 58
SASE life cycle 55
SASE management 91
  overview 86-88
SASE Monitoring Policy 58, 60
SASE Notification Policy 58
SASE Policy 57, 58, 97
SASE Policy End Point 58
SASE quality 59
SASE Security Functions Policy 58
SASE Security Policy 58
SASE service 77, 82
  components, identifying 45
  core services 79
  defining 44
  expanse 81, 82
  in flight 47-49
  options 79-81
  overview 78, 79
  requirements 46, 47
  roles functionality, identifying 46
  roles, identifying 46
SASE service on-demand 13
SASE services framework 22
SASE Session 51, 52, 59
  building, steps 52
SASE session flow 54
SASE Session Forwarding Policy 58, 60
SASE stakeholders 96
SASE Subscriber Policy 58, 60
SASE success 25
  defining 26
SASE templates 90
SASE term 157
SASE trust 61

SASE UNI 53
Scrum 15
Scrum Sprint Cycles 5
SD-SASE 39
Secure Access Service Edge (SASE)
    35, 44, 82, 110, 141
  automating 32
  defining 3, 4, 64
  embracing 7, 8
  Forward Concept 146, 147
  Forward Future 144
  Forward Measured 145, 146
  Forward Overview 142, 143
  Forward Present 143, 144
  integration 30
  manual method 27, 28
  market challenge 5, 6
  market evaluation 4
  orchestrate 30-32
  presenting 8
  reference link 3
  services 4
  templating process 28, 29
  value proposition, evaluating 6, 7
Secure AI operations 44
Secure Domain Name System
    Proxy (SDNSP) 74
Secure Domain Name System (SDNS) 48
Secure Web Gateway (SWG) 4, 72
security
  automation 75
  details 73, 74
  overview 72, 73
  sessions 74, 75
  summarizing 76
Security Information and Event
    Management (SIEM) 30, 72

Security Operations Center (SOC) 44, 72
Security Service Edge (SSE) 81
self-manage SASE 19, 20
Service Level Agreement (SLA) 22, 52, 59, 87
Service Level Management 25, 87
service management platform 24, 87
service orchestration 86
Single Sign-On (SSO) sessions 54
situation identity 66, 67
slide format, SASE
  connectivity 10
  framework 8
  future 10
  identity 9
  introduction 8
  managed service 8, 9
  policies 10
  security 9
  sessions 9
  situation 9
  stakeholders 9
  subscriber 9
  use cases 10
Software-as-a-Service (SaaS) 97
Software Defined Networking (SDN) 125
Software-Defined (SD) 36
Software-Defined Wide Area Network
    (SD-WAN) 3, 17, 35, 36, 77, 103, 149
  design 151, 152
  experience 154, 155
  failure 153, 154
  need for 37
  overview 150, 151
  practice 155, 156
  usage 38
  using, scenario 39

Software-Defined Wide Area Network (SD-WAN), solution components
  controllers 151
  edges 150
  gateways 150
  orchestrators 151

Software Development combined with Security and IT Operations (DevSecOps) 5, 16

sprint cycle 12

SSL/TLS 81

stakeholders
  business 96, 97
  overview 96
  success criteria 99
  technical stakeholders 97, 98
  user experiences (UX) 98

subject actor 45, 53

Subject Matter Expert (SME) 142, 143

T

target actor 45, 53

technical SASE Service 97

technical stakeholders 97, 98

U

URL Filtering (URLF) 74

use case 101, 102
  components 106
  examples 103-105
  insight 103
  value propositions 107, 108

use case design 105
  components 106
  examples 105
  policy design 106, 107

User Experience (UX) 3, 14, 20, 59, 89, 112

User Network Interface (UNI) 53

V

Virtual Machine (VM) 5

Virtual Network (VNet) function 5

W

Web Application Firewall (WAF) 72

what statement 106

when statement 106

where statement 106

who statement 106

why statement 106

Z

Zero Access 96

Zero Trust Architecture (ZTA) 78, 118

Zero Trust Framework (ZTF) 38, 44, 51, 58, 63, 78, 82, 117, 136, 143
  access 121
  components 118, 119
  feed 120
  overview 118
  solution 121

Zero Trust Network Access (ZTNA) 4, 104, 105, 118

Zero Trust (ZT) 78, 96

ZTF-based design 110

Packt.com

Subscribe to our online digital library for full access to over 7,000 books and videos, as well as industry leading tools to help you plan your personal development and advance your career. For more information, please visit our website.

Why subscribe?

- Spend less time learning and more time coding with practical eBooks and Videos from over 4,000 industry professionals
- Improve your learning with Skill Plans built especially for you
- Get a free eBook or video every month
- Fully searchable for easy access to vital information
- Copy and paste, print, and bookmark content

Did you know that Packt offers eBook versions of every book published, with PDF and ePub files available? You can upgrade to the eBook version at packt.com and as a print book customer, you are entitled to a discount on the eBook copy. Get in touch with us at customercare@packtpub.com for more details.

At www.packt.com, you can also read a collection of free technical articles, sign up for a range of free newsletters, and receive exclusive discounts and offers on Packt books and eBooks.

Other Books You May Enjoy

If you enjoyed this book, you may be interested in these other books by Packt:

Microsoft Defender for Cloud Cookbook

Sasha Kranjac

ISBN: 9781801076135

- Understand Microsoft Defender for Cloud features and capabilities
- Understand the fundamentals of building a cloud security posture and defending your cloud and on-premises resources
- Implement and optimize security in Azure, multi-cloud and hybrid environments through the single pane of glass - Microsoft Defender for Cloud
- Harden your security posture, identify, track and remediate vulnerabilities
- Improve and harden your security and services security posture with Microsoft Defender for Cloud benchmarks and best practices
- Detect and fix threats to services and resources

Check Point Firewall Administration R81.10+

Vladimir Yakovlev

ISBN: 9781801072717

- Understand various Check Point implementation scenarios in different infrastructure topologies
- Perform initial installation and configuration tasks using Web UI and the CLI
- Create objects of different categories and types
- Configure different NAT options
- Work with access control policies and rules
- Use identity awareness to create highly granular rules
- Operate high-availability clusters

Packt is searching for authors like you

If you're interested in becoming an author for Packt, please visit `authors.packtpub.com` and apply today. We have worked with thousands of developers and tech professionals, just like you, to help them share their insight with the global tech community. You can make a general application, apply for a specific hot topic that we are recruiting an author for, or submit your own idea.

Hi!

I am Jeremiah Ginn, the author of *Diving into Secure Access Service Edge*. I really hope you enjoyed reading this book and found it useful for increasing your ability to leverage SASE in your organization.

It would really help me (and other potential readers!) if you could leave a review on Amazon sharing your thoughts on *Diving into Secure Access Service Edge*.

Go to the link below or scan the QR code to leave your review:

`https://packt.link/r/1803242175`

Your review will help me to understand what's worked well in this book, and what could be improved upon for future editions, so it really is appreciated.

Best Wishes,

Jeremiah C. Ginn

Download a free PDF copy of this book

Thanks for purchasing this book!

Do you like to read on the go but are unable to carry your print books everywhere?

Is your eBook purchase not compatible with the device of your choice?

Don't worry, now with every Packt book you get a DRM-free PDF version of that book at no cost.

Read anywhere, any place, on any device. Search, copy, and paste code from your favorite technical books directly into your application.

The perks don't stop there, you can get exclusive access to discounts, newsletters, and great free content in your inbox daily

Follow these simple steps to get the benefits:

1. Scan the QR code or visit the link below

https://packt.link/free-ebook/9781803242170

2. Submit your proof of purchase
3. That's it! We'll send your free PDF and other benefits to your email directly

Made in the USA
Columbia, SC
19 September 2023